TABLE OF CONTENTS

INTRODUCTION

Overview

The driving of police vehicles on public roads attracts close scrutiny. The highest standards are expected from the police service and from individual officers, police staff and community volunteers at all times. It is recognised police drivers often perform their duties in stressful and demanding circumstances, but we are expected and must endeavour to, set a good example to other road users regardless of the nature of any particular incident or role in which police vehicles are being used. We also have a duty of care to ensure the safety of the public we serve, as well as the safety of our own staff at all times.

This document sits beside the College of Policing 'Police driving' Authorised Professional Practice (APP). It details force procedure in relation to the driving and use of police vehicles by employees and volunteers of Police, it takes account of:

> Revision of the previous Driving and Use of Police Vehicles Procedure.
> Current law.
> The addition of Police volunteers driving authorisation
> Implementation of Section19 of the Road Safety Act 2006.
> College of Policing APP in relation to Police Pursuits, Police Driving, and the Roads Policing and Police Driving Learning Programme (RPPDLP) .
> Current national occupational standards, guidance and recommendations relative to driver training.
> Our duty to effectively manage occupational road risk and health & safety, whilst retaining operational capability to meet the many competing demands placed upon the force and its drivers.
> Regular requests from staff to clarify what level of driving permit or training is required to drive vehicles in certain roles - and whether any restrictions apply.
> The National Decision Making model (NDM).

Limitations

This procedure does not cover the following:

- Reporting, recording and investigation of police road traffic collisions.
- Police Pursuits procedure.
- Roads Policing and Police Driving Learning Programme (RPPDLP) drivers handbook (DTU)

GLOSSARY OF TERMS

Term	Meaning
ACPO	Association of Chief Police Officers
AFO	Authorised Firearms Officer
APP	Authorised Professional Practice
ARV	Armed Response Vehicle
CBM	Community Beat Manager
CIU	Collision Investigation Unit
DCT	Dedicated Crime Team
DRA	Dynamic Risk Assessment
DVSA	Driver and Vehicle Standards Agency
DTU	Driving Training Unit
ECC	Emergency Communications Centre
FOM	Faculty of Occupational Medicine
NPCC	National Police Chiefs Council
PCSO's	Police Community Support Officers
PNLD	Police National Legal Database
FOWDER	System when checking vehicle (Fuel, Oil, Water, Damage, Electrics, Rubber – tyres – including spare - and windscreen wipers).
PSD	Professional Standards Dept.
RMU	Resource Management Unit

RP	Roads Policing
SB	Special Branch
SCD	Specialist Crime Directorate
SFC/TFC	Strategic Firearm Commander/ Tactical Firearm Commander
TFU	Tactical Firearms Unit
TPAC	Tactical Pursuit and Containment
TSU	Technical Support Unit

AUTHORISED PROFESSIONAL PRACTICE AREAS

Road Policing > Police Pursuits; Police Driving

DATA PROTECTION

Any information relating to an identified or identifiable living individual recorded as a consequence of this procedure will be processed in accordance with the Data Protection Act 2018, General Data Protection Regulations and the Force Data Protection Policy.

FREEDOM OF INFORMATION ACT 2000

This document has been assessed as suitable for public release.

MONITORING and REVIEW

This procedure will be reviewed tri-annually. A shorter review period will be implemented if required in the light of future developments and any relevant NPCC Guidance / APP.

WHO TO CONTACT ABOUT THIS PROCEDURE

The Persons responsible for this Procedure are:

Mr R Ward - Manager Driver Training Unit.
Inspector Freeman – Police Road Safety Unit Procedure Owner.
Mr John Gay - Vehicle Fleet Manager.

Either of the above may be contacted via e mail or internal telephone.

PURPOSE, RESPONSIBILITY AND OBLIGATIONS - DRIVING AT WORK (POLICE EMPLOYMENT).

Application

This procedure applies to all Police authority owned vehicles and staff or volunteers who drive at or in connection with work, to and from work, or for purposes authorised for community volunteers - no matter how infrequently.

The driver of <u>any</u> police authority owned vehicle must have the correct driver assessment or training and the appropriate authorisation in the form of a current driving permit, to be adequately equipped to safely drive vehicles to the standard their individual roles demand of them. This equally applies to hired, leased or loaned vehicles. In addition all drivers who drive on the force's insurance require authorisation to drive police authority owned vehicles or those hired, leased or loaned for the purposes of police work.

In the case of community volunteers and Police Staff there is no requirement for an assessment for unmarked 'grey fleet' basic vehicles. This also includes the community volunteer marked car due to the marking clearly showing it to be 'community volunteer'. (NB: this does not include vans, personnel carriers or exhibition vehicles)

Drivers (Volunteers, Police Staff or Police Officers) must <u>either</u> possess a current force driver permit authorising them to drive a particular category of vehicle in the role their current post demands, or be undergoing either a formal driver training course or driving assessment with the DTU to gain, regain, or extend their driver permit authorisation.

For the purposes of this document the term Police Officer shall include Special Constabulary officers.

Purpose of this Procedure

To determine which types of vehicle, whether owned by, leased or hired on behalf of Police, can be driven by individual staff and in what role - whether serving police officers, community volunteers or members of police staff.

It has been formulated solely to establish and maintain a reasonable, practical, safe and responsible approach to our driving activities - and to assist the force to discharge its legal responsibilities and duty of care to operate a safe system of work and, in particular, effectively manage occupational road risk.

Employee Obligations, Personal Responsibility and Use of Private Vehicles

Before driving any vehicle on the public highway during the course of their employment, employees/ volunteers <u>must</u> possess a full DVLA licence for that class of vehicle which permits them to do so. If they are in <u>any</u> doubt, they must not drive the vehicle and take advice if necessary from either, the Fleet Manager or the DTU. DVLA driving licence queries can also be researched direct via their website facilities.

The force must manage its own obligations robustly and consequently the following will apply: Prior to any driving permit being issued, staff/volunteers will be required to produce their DVLA driving licence and undergo a eyesite test. The DTU will conduct the eyesite test and assess the DVLA driving licence.

At the commencement of any driving assessment or driving course, staff will be required to produce their DVLA driving licence to a member of the DTU.

Any employee who is disqualified from driving, or has their driving licence revoked (for any reason) **must** disclose this to line management **without delay.** (See also "Reportable Matters" below).

All staff have a legal responsibility to ensure their own private vehicles are roadworthy if used on the public roads. In respect of Insurance, if used in the course of employment, then your vehicle or any other private vehicle you are using, must have insurance that covers this (as opposed to just travelling to and from work each day). This will mean in most cases insuring the vehicle for "Business Use". **If anyone is in any doubt they should check this with their insurance company.**

In the event of a Police Officer, member of Police Staff or Community Volunteer being involved in an RTC whilst driving for Police purposes they will still be legally obligated to advise their insurance companies of this regardless of where the liability of the incident lies.

The only exception to this are Police Officer Advanced Drivers engaged in a TPAC boxing in manoeuvre where it is accepted there may be contact made between vehicles.

Staff/volunteers also have a legal responsibility to ensure they do not drive when they have a medical condition that should have been declared to DVLA and has not been. Failure to notify DVLA is a criminal offence.

No member of staff should drive in contravention of professional medical advice received. Employees who drive in connection with work have a personal responsibility to disclose any restrictions or concerns they have regarding their fitness to drive to their line manager, who will take necessary steps to ensure safety is not compromised. Advice can be taken from Occupational Health, HR and line management as necessary in the individual circumstances. (Further information can be found in the "Medical Standards - Drivers" section of this procedure and within the police driving APP).

Staff who simply feel unwell at work on any particular occasion or excessively fatigued - and do not feel well enough or able to drive, or are concerned about safely driving themselves, must take personal responsibility and inform their line manager as a matter of welfare and personal/public safety.

In addition to the provisions of road traffic legislation, any supervisor having reasonable grounds to do so, may request and will be permitted to inspect, the Driving Licence, Insurance, MOT and Vehicle Registration Document for any private vehicle owned or used by any member of staff in connection with work, or to travel to and from work, at any reasonable time. He or she shall outline their grounds to the member of staff at the time of making any such request. If the member of staff does not have their documents with them at that time, they will produce them for inspection as soon as practicable.

The College of Policing Code of Ethics along with the Schedule to the Police (Conduct) Regulations 2008, sets out standards of professional behaviour expected of police officers and members of the Special Constabulary. Standards of professional behaviour includes that which discredits the police service or can undermine public confidence in it, whether on or off duty. Requirements for Police Staff in effect mirror those for police officers in respect of disclosure of any action taken against them for a criminal offence, any condition imposed on them by a court, or the receipt of any penalty notice. The expectation is that Community Volunteers shall also adopt the same personal responsibility.

Reportable Matters: Police Officers, Police Staff (On or Off Duty), Community Volunteers

In consequence of the above, Police Officers, Police Staff and Community Volunteers are required to report as soon as reasonably practicable to Professional Standards Department (PSD) any occasion in the UK or elsewhere when they have been:

1. Subject to arrest*
2. Served with a summons for an offence*
3. Issued with a penalty notice for disorder*
4. Issued with an endorsable fixed penalty notice for a road traffic offence*
5. Charged with an offence by an enforcement agency*
6. Cautioned for an offence by an enforcement agency*
7. Convicted of an offence*
8. Sentenced*
9. Given conditions imposed by any court*

* The offences above relate to **any** offence, not just Road Traffic Offences, although in the context of this Procedure, the focus is upon those offences above which relate to driving and vehicles - whether police authority or privately owned, or hired/leased.

Such reports must be in writing to their Management Team for the attention of PSD.

Aside and separate from any other considerations/action, this procedure requires occupational road risk be managed effectively. Each individual case must therefore be risk assessed regarding continuing safety to drive vehicles to the standard the individual's role demands of them. To ensure consistency of application and continuity in this regard, the designated officer responsible for the review of Police Collisions (POLCOL) in force will consider driving related remedial action in each case.

In appropriate cases, pending remedial action, he/she will consider suspension of the driver from driving or restrict their driver permit (for example to non immediate response driving), as a necessary control measure. This will not prevent another supervisor or manager from suspending a driver from driving police vehicles until such time as the 'designated officer' has reviewed the matter and made his/her decision. (See later sections on "Remedial Action and Penalty Points" in this procedure). Following this a proportionate response will be considered to address the situation.

Professional Standards related enquiries in relation to the above should be addressed to PSD. Line management will consider the wider consequences of any disqualification or revocation of an individual's driving licence and consider appropriate action in each individual case. HR will be consulted if necessary in the particular circumstances.

DRIVER PERMIT AUTHORISATION AND VEHICLE CLASSIFICATION LEVELS

NB: It is important the contents of the previous section are noted and all staff are aware of their obligations and personal responsibilities in relation to, not only driving police authority owned vehicles, but also their own private vehicles as well.

Classification of Drivers & Vehicles

Drivers are categorised according to their level of training or assessment to meet the requirements of their individual current role. The level of driver training and authorisation to perform various roles is set against the vehicle classification. The relationship between the two is detailed in the table below.

Police operate a diverse fleet of vehicles produced by a range of manufacturers. These vehicles are procured by the Vehicle Fleet Manager (VFM) to meet operational needs as identified by Senior Management. Working to the Force Fleet Strategy, the VFM will also consider appropriate guidance issued periodically, including by the Home Office. Vehicles are then classified by the VFM based upon a combination of their intended operational role, their performance and their attributes in response to national recommendations and best practice.

All drivers (Volunteers, police and police staff) require a driving permit if they have to drive police authority owned, hired or leased vehicles as part of their role within the force, even if this is infrequent. See the tables below which are intended as a quick reference guide and also the section on Driver Permits (page 31) for further details.

Table: Driver Permit and Vehicle Classification Levels

Driver Permit Classification	Role & Driver Training or Assessment Level Required	Can Drive Vehicle Classification
"Authorised only"	SPECIALIST VEHICLES - details specified on individual permits eg, PSU vehs, Motorcycles (Std & Advanced), DTU vehs, Trailers, Medium & Large Goods Vehicles, etc	"Authorised only"
9	TPAC	9
8	ADVANCED CAR	8
7	NOT CURRENTLY USED	7
6	STANDARD RESPONSE - HOSTYDS TRAINED	5
5	STANDARD RESPONSE	5
4	POLICE BASIC - STOP VEHICLES	3
3	POLICE BASIC	3
2	PCSO - POLICE BASIC ASSESSMENT	2
1	POLICE STAFF / VOLUNTEER (grey fleet/marked volunteer car) – NO ASSESSMENT [NB: Vans/personel carrier/exhibition vehicle – an assessment will be required].	1

The practical distinctions between the different driver categories have been put in place in recognition of individual specialist driver training and skills necessary to perform particular operational roles and engage in certain approved driving tactics, required as part of modern day policing.

This essential demarcation enables drivers to drive any class of vehicle in its intended operational policing role, provided:

- they have received the required driving training and
- they are authorised to perform the role (by Line Management) and
- they possess a current driving permit authorisation.

As an illustration of the above, any driver who for example, has a current permit classification of 8, can drive vehicles with a vehicle classification that corresponds with 8 in the table above, or any vehicle below that in its intended operational policing role.

This does not prevent a driver being authorised by a Line Manager to drive a particular vehicle of a higher classification from "A to B", ie not in its intended operational role, for example to go and take a statement or conduct an enquiry. They cannot be authorised to perform any role above their current driver training level or authorisation and must not do so. A practical example would be that a basic trained driver cannot perform the role of a response driver and/or drive using blue lights and sirens, or claim speed limit exemptions in the process. To be able to do this, the individual would require a standard response driver training course and gain a current driver permit classification of 5.

In summary - no driver should either be deployed or engage in, any operational role or tactic for which he or she has not been trained and is currently authorised.

The table starting on page 17 sets out the different vehicle types in force, their use and summarises the requirements for drivers to use them in their intended role. Further sections of this procedure provide supporting guidance and information eg, Driver Permits.

Vehicle and User Classification Marks

As a control measure, all police authority owned vehicles will be physically labelled according to the vehicles approved use and permit requirements - to which the table above refers.

Each marked police vehicle will display a classification number(s) as an identification aide to help ensure non authorised driving/use does not occur. The classification number will appear on the driver's side window and in the vehicle log book.

For unmarked vehicles the vehicle classification will be indicated in or on the vehicle log book. Vehicles intended for surveillance operations will be marked in such a way so as not to compromise the vehicle.

A typical example of a classification mark in the form of a windscreen sticker is shown in the example below.

VEHICLE DRIVER CLASSIFICATION
OPERATIONAL WITH SIRENS
5
OPERATIONAL WITHOUT SIRENS
3
NON-OPERATIONAL
1

"Operational" - allows the driver to use the vehicle in its intended operational role - in this case as a response vehicle, using blue lights and sirens with eligibility to claim speed exemptions - assuming the driver has authorisation to drive that vehicle and a current driving permit of 5 or above to support this. General patrol in a vehicle will be deemed as 'operational'.

"Non-operational" - to be interpreted in the strictest sense. Enables **occasional** use of the vehicle outside of its intended operational role, eg, to go and take a statement, conduct an enquiry or facilitate the general movement of the vehicle eg, from 'A' to 'B', e.g. for servicing. Any member of staff with a driver permit classification of 1 could drive the vehicle in these circumstances, provided they had authorisation to do so. This would not cover emergency response driving or permit the driver exemption from statutory speed limits.

Following the implementation of Section19 of the Road Safety Act 2006 police officers and members of police staff **cannot** claim speed exemptions **unless** they have been trained to drive at high speed. For the police service this will equate to current authorised standard response level drivers as a minimum.

The Vehicle Fleet Manager will be responsible for ensuring each vehicle is classified and marked correctly.

Categories of police vehicle (as per APP)

The National Association of Police Fleet Managers (NAPFM) and the College of Policing use a calculated assessment to determine a vehicles overall performance which deliveries a final Performance Value (PV) enabling categorisation of Response and Advanced cars, Motorcycles, and Vans up to 3.5t.

An explanation of the assessment and calculation method can be found within APP.

Performance Values

Cars and Vans (up to 3.5 t)

Category	Response	Advanced
Performance Value (PV)	3.2 PV and above	Below 3.2 PV

Vehicle Classification Records

The Vehicle Fleet Manager will maintain a record of the classification of every vehicle in the fleet and will make the record available to Management upon request.

Vehicle Re-Classification Records

Senior Management may wish a particular vehicle's classification to be considered for amendment as a consequence of experience or operational need. This will be referred to the Fleet Manager who will decide based upon the individual circumstances and will ensure that a record of the decision is retained. In cases where there is any disagreement, the matter will be referred to the Force Driver Training Lead who will make the final decision.

Urgent Emergency Operational Need

In circumstances where due to **urgent emergency operational necessity** a driver needs to use a police vehicle other than that for which they are authorised, the member of staff may drive that vehicle on the authority of a CIM/FIM (See * below). Such authority will allow the use of that vehicle only to the extent required to deal with the particular incident or task in hand.

In these circumstances, drivers **may not** use the vehicle in an emergency response role or mode (blue lights and/or sirens), or exceed speed limits/claim legal exemptions, **unless** they are currently trained to do so for that category of vehicle. This means the driver has either successfully passed a standard response driving course or response driving assessment in the last 5 years or, the advanced driving equivalent of either of the above (whichever is required for the vehicle in question).

Whenever a CIM/FIM* decides to authorise any member of police staff to use a police vehicle in such circumstances, the authorising officer must be able to justify their decision on the grounds of urgent emergency operational necessity and proportionality.

{* In the case of an RP Vehicle (only), an RP Supervisor can authorise the above, in which case to use blue lights and/or sirens, exceed speed limits/claim legal exemptions, or pursue vehicles which fail to stop - the driver must be <u>Advanced level</u> as a minimum}.

CIM's/FIM's (or RP Supervisors where applicable) are advised to record their decision and the grounds.

No member of police staff can be authorised by another to drive or use a police vehicle illegally, i.e., authorising someone to drive a vehicle outside of the legal limitations of their personal DSA driving licence, e.g., driving a personnel carrier/PSU vehicle that has between 9 and 16 passenger seats - if that person does not have a Category D1 entitlement on their licence.

In the same vein, the implementation of Section19 of the Road Safety Act 2006, means police officers and members of police staff **cannot** claim speed exemptions **unless** they have been trained and in date to drive at high speed. For the police service this will equate to current authorised standard response level drivers as a minimum.

RP Aides and New AFO's

RP Aides and new AFO's must possess a current advanced driver permit before they can drive RP and ARV's - unless the purpose is <u>non</u>-operational <u>and</u> will not involve either

- emergency response mode driving
- exercising legal exemptions or
- pursuit of vehicles

Patrol work will always be considered to be operational work.

New RP/AFO Sergeants and Inspectors

As per RP Aides and new AFO's above.

WHO CAN DRIVE WHAT VEHICLE IN WHAT ROLE?

Overview

It is recognised operational force requirements regarding vehicle acquisition and their operational roles can change. If anyone is in any doubt as to whether they possess either the correct DVLA driving licence category, or correct force driving permit to drive a particular vehicle for their required role, they must not drive the vehicle until they have checked this out. Appropriate advice is available from either, the Fleet Manager, the DTU or an RP colleague. DVLA driving licence queries can also be researched direct via their website facilities.

Servicing/General Movement of Vehicles

When the need arises, restricted (non-operational) use of vehicles, e.g., driving from "A to B" for servicing/ general movement of vehicles is permitted by staff, provided they possess the relevant DVLA driving licence permitting them to drive the vehicle, they have authority to do so - and they possess a minimum driving permit of level1 (police staff basic).

Note Regarding Speed Exemptions (Road Safety Act).

Following the implementation of <u>Section 19 Road Safety Act 2006</u>, police officers/ police staff/ Community Volunteers **cannot** claim speed exemptions **unless** they have been trained to drive at high speed. For the police service this equates to current authorised standard response level drivers as a minimum.

Pursuit Procedure - Unmarked Vehicles

Current trained Response Drivers are trained in Initial Stage Pursuits. All drivers must be aware of <u>APP Road Policing > Police Pursuits</u> and the <u>National TPAC Tactics Directory</u> [NB: you need to be logged into MLE/NCALT to access the Tactics Directory].

An important notification with regard to the use of unmarked vehicles in pursuits was circulated to Chief Inspectors on 28/11/2013 by the Head of RPU at the time, with a request it be forwarded to Inspectors "who ultimately manage staff &/or pursuits depending on their role" to "make them fully aware of the new policy....". The ACC, Fleet Manager and DTU Manager were all sighted. An extract reads as follows:

"the policy makes it clear that only "Unmarked cars fitted with audible and visual warning equipment which are driven by suitably trained drivers and deemed fit for use in Tactical Phase Pursuit" can be used. This means that only Tactically Trained (TPAC) Drivers can conduct both an Initial & Tactical Phase pursuit in an unmarked vehicle, Tactical Grade vehicles are high powered and are only operated by RPU, SCIT, ARG, DCT & SCD. This is a change from the previous policy in that historically we allowed Standard Trained drivers to conduct initial phase pursuits in unmarked response graded vehicles, this practice must stop from this date forward. This is not negotiable and has been agreed nationally by ACPO (NPCC)".

Summary Table

The table below is intended as a quick reference guide by vehicle type - in relation to "who can drive what vehicle in what role". Other sections of this procedure provide supporting guidance and information eg, the section on Driver Permits:

Vehicle Type	Vehicle Use/Guidance	Driver Requirements
Roads Policing Patrol (Fast Roads) Vehicles (RP)	Advanced vehicles. Fitted with blue lights and sirens. Either marked (liveried) or unmarked. May be 4 x4 drive eg, BMW X5. For RP duties & suitable for motorway patrol /fast roads deployment. Certain RP issue vehicles capable of heavyweight utility off-road use eg; Land Rover Discovery or future similar spec vehicles. • Land Rover Discoveries are not fit for Tactical Phase Pursuits. All vehicles issued for RP duties will have a vehicle classification of 8.	**Police Officers** Must be advanced level with a current minimum driver permit classification of 8 and posted to either RP,RSU, AFO, DCT/ DST or the DTU Alternatively to the above Driver has been authorised by an RP Supervisor to drive the vehicle (see Urgent Operational Need p15 above). (In which case must drive within the limitations of their driving permit. In the case of a standard driver, they will not however be authorised to • drive in emergency response mode • pursue vehicles which fail to stop or • exercise legal exemptions). TM Police Staff may drive vehicles from A to B e.g. to and from events including towing if required under classification 1. They are not allowed to drive the vehicle beyond the guidelines of that classification. **PCSO's** Not currently permitted to drive these vehicles. If force requirements change in the future, the operational driver permit requirement **must** correspond to that of police officers above.

Vehicle Type	Vehicle Use/Guidance	Driver Requirements
Armed Response Vehicles	Advanced vehicles. Fitted with blue lights and sirens. Either marked or unmarked. May be 4 x4 drive eg BMW X5 For AFO duties & suitable for motorway patrol / deployment. Vehicle classification 8.	**Police Officers** Drivers must be advanced level with a current driver permit classification of 8. • Member of Specialist Ops SLT (requirements of forthcoming Road Safety Act to be complied with). Alternatively to the above - the driver has been authorised by an AFO Supervisor to drive the vehicle. (In which case they must drive within the limitations of their driving permit). In the case of a standard driver they will not be authorised to • drive in emergency response mode • pursue vehicles which fail to stop • exercise legal exemptions.
Response Vehicles	For operational emergency response. Fitted with blue lights and sirens. Normally marked (liveried). In some cases may be unmarked at discretion of Fleet manager. Response duties will be performed in marked response vehicles where possible, to reduce risks by maximising visibility to other road users. Unmarked response vehicles should not be routinely used where marked response vehicles are available. Can be 4 wheel drive - manual or fully auto gearbox with high/low ratios or difflock, & increased ground clearance, eg Vauxhall Antara or equivalent. Suitable for lightweight off-road use ("green lanes" etc - not suitable for "heavyweight" full off-road cross country use). {Current issue Dog Section and Prisoner Handling vans are both suitable for responding to emergencies. See Van section (pages 24-25 below}. Vehicle classification for Response Duties level 5.	**Police Officers** For emergency response (blue lights & sirens) and eligibility to claim speed exemptions, a current driver permit level 5 is required. As above.

Vehicle Type	Vehicle Use/Guidance	Driver Requirements
Response Vehicles (cont)	**Note 1.** Response vehicles can be used by Basic level trained drivers, incl Special Constabulary & PCSO's, but these should be marked vehicles for routine policing/patrol/stop checks to reduce risks - including when stationary at a scene on the highway. Drivers **cannot** be authorised to drive in emergency response role using blue lights and sirens, or be eligible to claim speed limit exemptions. (PCSO's have no power to stop vehicles). **Note 2.** In the absence of a current standard driving permit level 5, drivers in Note1 above are **not** authorised to use the emergency response equipment (but see note 3. below). exceed speed limits {see note above this table re speed exemptions/ Road Safety Act implications}. 'follow' vehicles that have failed to stop. engage in pursuits at any stage and (unless permit classification 4), attempt to stop members of the motoring public whilst driving. **Note 3**. May operate the vehicle's blue lights whilst stationary at the scene of an incident, if considered necessary to warn others of an obstruction in the highway, or to assist in protecting a scene.	**In Non Emergency Response Mode:** **Police Drivers, Special Constabulary & PCSO's.** Notes 1-3 opposite apply. Driver permit minimum classification of **1** (police staff) and **3** (police officers/special constables). Permit classification 4 is the minimum for stopping vehicles (police officer/special constables only).
CPT Vehicles **(now upgraded to Response level)**	CPT vehicles are all response graded vehicles fitted with blue lights & sirens. Driver permit requirements for emergency response driving in the adjacent column are unchanged. Vehicles will be marked. Vehicle classification will reflect the grade/spec of the particular vehicle. **Note 1.** Notes 2 and 3 under "response vehicles" section above apply.	All Staff - whether Police Officers, Special Constables, PCSO's or other staff. Driver permit minimum classification of 1 (police staff) and 3 (police officers/special constables). Permit classification 4 is the minimum for stopping vehicles (police officer/special constables only). Drivers **cannot** be authorised to drive any vehicle in emergency response mode using blue lights and

Vehicle Type	Vehicle Use/Guidance	Driver Requirements
		sirens, and/or be eligible to claim speed limit exemptions, **unless** trained to standard level with a current minimum driver permit classification of 5. {For speed exemptions/implications of Road Safety Act - see note above this table}.
CID Vehicles	Lower powered Unmarked. Not fit for purpose for emergency response driving or duties. For MIT, general CID duties - use as required for enquiries, appointments & other general purpose tasks. Vehicle classification 1.	All Staff - whether Police Officers, Special Constables, PCSO's or other Staff Driver permit minimum classification of 1/2 (police staff/volunteers) and 3 (police officers/special constables). Drivers **cannot** be authorised to drive any vehicle in emergency response mode using blue lights and sirens, and/or be eligible to claim speed limit exemptions, **unless** trained to standard level with a current minimum driver permit classification of 5. {For speed exemptions/implications of Road Safety Act - see note above this table}.
DCT Patrol Vehicles	• Resonse or Advanced vehicles Can be marked or unmarked. Fitted with blue lights and sirens. For DCT duties. If Advanced <u>and</u> carrying full kit to motorway std, then suitable for motorway patrol / deployment. Vehicle Classification 5 or 8	High Powered Vehicles: Advanced level - current minimum driver permit classification of 8 or Response Vehicles: Standard level (min) - current driver permit classification of 5. To drive within speed limits, ie to normal DVSA driving test standard without the need to claim statutory speed exemptions - driver requires a permit minimum classification of **1** (police staff) and **3** (police officers/special constables). However if the situation demands, or is likely to demand, the driver having to exceed speed limits and be eligible to claim speed exemptions, then whether or not the vehicle's blue lights & sirens are used, the driver cannot do this and is not eligible to claim an exemption - unless trained to at least standard level with a <u>current minimum</u> driver training classification of 5.

Vehicle Type	Vehicle Use/Guidance	Driver Requirements
	Also low powered vehicles, not fitted with blue lights/sirens. Not suitable for "emergency response" driving & not used for other than normal driving within posted speed limits. For enquiries, appointments & other routine non -emergency tasks. Vehicle Classification 1	For low powered Vehicles - driver permit minimum classification of 1 (police staff) and 3 (police officers/special constables).

SCD Vehicles (Excluding Motorcycles)	Resonse or advanced vehicles. Unmarked.
	Fitted with covert blue lights and sirens.
	Unmarked vehicles
	    Suitable for operating (in SCD role - incl surveillance operations) on all roads.
	Not suitable for deployment to operational incident on motorway as insufficient kit carried).
	Surveillance vehicles have their classification marked in such a way so as not to compromise the vehicle.
	Unmarked.
	Fitted with covert blue lights and sirens.
		Advanced level - current minimum driver permit classification of 8.
		Response Vehicles:
		    Standard level (min) - current driver permit classification of 5.
		<u>All mobile surveillance trained drivers are also trained to advanced level.</u>
		To drive within speed limits, ie to normal DSA driving test standard without the need to claim statutory speed exemptions - driver requires a driving permit minimum classification of 1 (police staff) and 3 (police officers).
		However if in the course of their duty the situation demands, or is likely to demand, the driver to exceed speed limits and be eligible to claim speed exemptions, then whether or not the vehicle's blue lights & sirens are used at this time, the driver cannot do this and is not eligible to claim an exemption - unless trained to at least standard level with a <u>current minimum</u> driver training classification of 5 (for response Vehicles) and 8 (if Advaced vehicles)
		
		    {For speed exemptions / implications of Road Safety Act - see note above this table}.
		
		Low powered Vehicles - driver permit minimum classification of **1** (police staff) and **3** (police officers/special constables).

	Also low powered vehicles, not fitted with blue lights/sirens. Not suitable for "emergency response" driving & not used for other than normal driving to within posted speed limits. For enquiries, appointments & other routine non -emergency tasks. Vehicle Classification 1	

Vehicle Type	Vehicle Use/Guidance	Driver Requirements
SCD Motorcycles (Surveillance work)	Moved to "Authorised Specialist Vehs" table below with other motorcycles in use in force).	Moved to "Authorised Specialist Vehs" table below with other motorcycles in use in force).
SB	Response or advanced vehicles. Unmarked. Resonse vehicles can be fitted with covert blue lights and sirens. For SB duties (which do not include mobile surveillance) Vehicle Classification 2 or 5 **Note1:** If mobile surveillance becomes necessary, this would require advanced trained drivers in suitable vehicles in line with SCD above, who currently conduct all mobile surveillance operations.	Driving permit minimum classification of **1** (police staff) and **3** (police officers) to drive within speed limits, ie to normal DVSA driving test standard without the need to claim statutory speed exemptions. To drive in emergency response mode using blue lights and sirens, and be eligible to claim speed limit exemptions, drivers **must** be at least standard level with a current driver permit classification of 5. • Mobile surveillance operations = surveillance trained drivers who are also trained advanced drivers in suitable vehicles.
SO 15 Response Vehicles	• Response vehicles. Unmarked. Fitted with covert blue lights and sirens. For SO15 duties Officers may be requiried to drive an SO15 vehicle (or another vehicle for SO15 duties) belonging to another force.Vice-versa could also apply. In either case, drivers must be suitably trained. Vehicle Classification 5 **Note1:** If mobile surveillance becomes necessary, this would require advanced trained drivers in suitable vehicles in line with SCD above, who currently conduct all mobile surveillance operations.	Driving permit minimum classification of 1 (police staff) and 3 (police officers) to drive from "A to B", eg to and from an incident, **without** the need to exercise statutory speed exemptions. • As per Response Vehicles ie To drive in emergency response mode using blue lights and sirens, and be eligible to claim speed limit exemptions, drivers **must** be at least standard level with a current driver permit classification of 5. • Mobile surveillance operations = surveillance trained drivers who are also trained advanced drivers in suitable vehicles.

Vehicle Type	Vehicle Use/Guidance	Driver Requirements
Vehicles Used by Duty Officers/ TFC/ Force Cover. Includes vehicles being used by <u>any</u> officer or member of police staff of any rank or position, for duty cover, or call out etc. eg TFC Silver Cadre, to get to/from an incident.	Response vehicles May be fitted with blue lights and sirens. Either marked (liveried) or unmarked Used for example by TFC Cadre, to get to/from an incident. Includes call out to an incident for any reason. **Note1:** In the absence of a current standard driving permit level 5, drivers are **not** authorised to use emergency response equipment (but see note 2. below) exceed speed limits 'follow' vehicles that have failed to stop engage in pursuits at any stage undertake surveillance driving and, (unless permit classification 4) attempt to stop members of the motoring public whilst driving. **Note 2**. May operate the vehicle's blue lights whilst stationary at the scene of an incident, if considered necessary to warn others of an obstruction in the highway, or to assist in protecting the scene.	Driving permit minimum classification of 1 (police staff) and 3 (police officers/special contables) to drive from "A to B", eg to and from an incident, **without** the need to exercise statutory speed exemptions. To drive in emergency response mode using blue lights and sirens, or be eligible to claim speed limit exemptions (whether or not blue lights and sirens are in use), drivers **must** be at least Standard level with a <u>current</u> minimum driver training classification of 5. <u>Above also applies if the driver is using a privately owned or hired vehicle for police purposes.</u> (Vehicles leased to staff covered under "Authorised Specialist Vehicles" in the table below). See notes 1 and 2 opposite - middle column. {For speed exemptions / implications of Road Safety Act - see note above this table}.
Chief Officers Team STAFF cars only **Vehicles Used by ACC rank or above OR the appointed Chief Constables driver**	• Advanced vehicles • Response vehicles • Used for example by designated Chief Officers driver to get to/from an incident. • Includes call out to an incident for any reason but may only use emergency lights and sirens if appropriately trained unless ACC or above. • Note 1 and 2 within TFC above also applies	• Advanced level – current permit minimum driver permit classification 8 • To drive in emergency response mode using blue lights and sirens, or be eligible to claim speed limit exemptions (whether or not blue lights and sirens are in use), drivers **must** be at least Standard level with a <u>current</u> minimum driver training classification of 5.
Pool Cars	Response vehicles. Not fitted with blue lights and sirens. Unmarked (non liveried). Non operational pool vehicles for use by staff, eg to get to/from appointments and events as part of their role, without need to exercise speed exemptions. Vehicle classification 1.	Driving permit classification of 1/2 (police staff/ volunteers) and 3 (police officers)

Vehicle Type	Vehicle Use/Guidance	Driver Requirements
Motorcycles - Marked (Liveried) See Middle Column.	{For Fleet Admin reasons, Motorcycle categorisation changed to "Specialist Vehicle". Both vehicle classification & rider permit classification now "Authorised Only}." For details/rider requirements - see "Specialist Vehicles" table below (starting on page 26).	As per adjacent middle column.
Vans (Excluding Personnel Carriers) **(Incl Prisoner Handling Vans & Dog Vans below).**	Marked or unmarked dependant upon role. If marked - may be fitted with blue lights & sirens - Fleet Manager will decide if particular vehicles are suitable for response/CIU role before fitment of both. For operational use (depending upon role & driver permit), by Response Officers, NPT, Special Constables, PCSO's, CIU, CSI's & members of TSU. For non operational use by police staff as required. Vehicle classification 1, 5 or 8 dependent upon intended role. **CSI vehicles fitted with blue lights:** Staff may only use blue lights whilst stationary at the scene of an incident if considered necessary to warn others of an obstruction in the highway, or to assist in protecting the scene.	<u>All Staff</u> <u>Reminder</u> - Ensure you possess the relevant current DVLA driving licence permitting you to drive the particular vehicle. (Fleet Mgr can advise on the specific requirement if advice required). <u>A separate driving assessment is required to drive vans.</u> This does **not** apply to current issue Dog Section and Prisoner Handling vans (eg, Peugeot / Mercedes Vito). **If in any doubt take advice from the DTU.** Driving permit classification minimum of 1 (police staff) and 3 (police officers / special constables). For emergency response (blue lights & sirens) and eligibility to claim speed exemptions, a <u>current</u> driver permit level 5 is required. Drivers who are not standard response level trained or above, may operate the vehicle's blue lights whilst stationary at the scene of an incident, if considered necessary to warn others of an obstruction in the highway, or to assist in protecting the scene. CIU use Advanced vans. Emergency CIU response requires drivers be advanced level - current minimum driver permit classification of 8. For emergency response (blue lights & sirens) and eligibility to claim speed exemptions, a <u>current</u> driver permit level 5 is required.
Prisoner Handling Vans (Eg, Mercedes Vito (or future similar spec approved by Fleet Mgr).	Marked (Liveried) Fitted with blue lights and sirens. Suitable for Response Duties & Prisoner Handling	For emergency response (blue lights & sirens) and eligibility to claim speed exemptions, a <u>current</u> driver permit level 5 is required. {For speed exemptions / implications of Road Safety Act - see note above this table}.

Vehicle Type	Vehicle Use/Guidance	Driver Requirements
Dog Vans For other "Specialist" Vehicles - see table below (starting on page 23).	Marked (Liveried) Fitted with blue lights and sirens. Suitable for Dog Section duties and & emergency response mode driving. For other "Specialist" Vehicles - see table below (starting on page 23).	For other "Specialist" Vehicles - see table below (starting on page 23).

Authorised Specialist Vehicles

A number of vehicles within the fleet are considered specialist vehicles and/or attract particular legal requirements in so far as driver licensing is concerned, eg, Personnel Carrier - or require specific assessment or instruction in order that they may be safely operated on the public highway.

The Vehicle Fleet Manager will be responsible in the first instance, for identifying and categorising these specialist vehicles taking into account their individual characteristics and, in conjunction with the DTU Manager, coming to a decision about the level of instruction and/or assessment required. The number of authorised specialist vehicles will be kept to a minimum and, wherever possible, a numeric vehicle classification will be utilised.

Any change in a recommended level of instruction or assessment will normally be decided by the DTU Manager in consultation with the Fleet Manager. In cases where there is any disagreement, the matter will be referred to the most appropriate manager to review the case (usually Force Ops Inspector) who will decide.

Individual permits will contain more detail - supplemented by the table on **page 11**. Further advice can be obtained from either the Fleet or DTU Managers as appropriate.

The vehicles in the table below are categorised as **Authorised Specialist Vehicles**:-

Authorised Specialist Vehicles

Vehicle Type	Vehicle Use/Guidance	Driver Requirements
Roads Policing (RP) Motorcycles - Marked (Liveried)	With the exception of off-road motorcycles used by RP (categorised below), the force only operate Advanced motorcycles. Fitted with blue lights & sirens. For operational use by staff (per right hand column), who have received the requisite rider training and therefore authorisation to do so. Vehicle classification "Authorised Only"	**RP Duties:** • Riders <u>must also</u> be current advanced drivers. <u>Minimum</u> standard motorcycle level with a current rider permit classification of "Authorised Only" **NB:** Legacy permits of classification 7 accepted <u>provided in-date </u>(ie last course/assessment **not** more than 5 years previously). Permit to be amended to "Authorised Only" after next m/cycle

Vehicle Type	Vehicle Use/Guidance	Driver Requirements
		assessment. Irrespective of above, force policy is to ensure RP motorcylists attain advanced rider status & maintain that level. Under the latest college of policing recommendations there will be only one police motorcycle course which will qualify the rider to advanced level. This recognises the particular vulnerability of motorcyclists to injury should a collision occur - and the additional safety margins gained, when riders successfully undergo motorcycle training to police advanced level. Once an RP officer obtains a standard motorcycle permit, they must complete an advanced course within 3 years (at the latest).*(Upon the introduction of the new police motorcycle course this section will not be relevant) Line management should initiate the necessary action for this to be managed and achieved as soon as practicable, taking into account the need to consolidate standard riding experience and prepare them for the advanced course. It is recognised not all students will pass the advanced course first time. Alongside this the force has a duty to manage occupational road risk effectively. Therefore if, despite several attempts (not explicitly defined but more than one) at the advanced course, the student consistently fails to achieve the level required for advanced motorcycle status, the DTU Manager and appropriate operational manager will review the student's suitability to continue performing RP motorcycle duties.
SCD Motorcycles (Surveillance work)	Advanced motorcycles Unmarked Fitted with covert blue lights and sirens. For surveillance duties. Vehicle Classification "Authorised Only". {For Fleet Admin reasons only, the previous vehicle	• All motorcycle riders must also be current advanced drivers. Riders must be advanced level with a current motorcyclist permit classification of "Authorised Only". {For Fleet Admin reasons only, the previous permit classification is changed, with **no** drop in required rider training standard}.

Vehicle Type	Vehicle Use/Guidance	Driver Requirements
	classification is changed}	**NB:** Legacy permits of classification 10 accepted provided in-date (ie last course/assessment **not** more than 5 years previously). Permit to be amended to "Authorised Only" following next m/cycle assessment.
Motorcycles - Dual Purpose Specialist On/Off Road Use (RP)	Response motorcycles (liveried) Fitted with blue lights & sirens Suitable for off road operational duties. For use by RP motorcyclists who are trained and authorised to ride such machines in an off road environment. Vehicle Classification "Authorised Only".	• All motorcycle riders must also be current advanced drivers. Will be trained and authorised to ride such machines in an off road environment. Rider permit classification of "Authorised Only"
Personnel Carrier (Unprotected ie Non PSU Specification)	Used in operational/non operational circumstances by: police officers, special constables, PCSO's and police staff, all of whom must be authorised to use these vehicles, ie, meet the driver requirements opposite. May be fitted with blue lights & sirens dependent upon role. Fleet Manager will decide on any such fitment. Vehicles classified within the "Specialist Vehicles" category "Authorised Only"	• Driver must possess Category D1 on their DVLA driving licence. (Drivers who passed their DVSA driving test on or after 1/1/97 do not have the D1 category automatically included and must pass a specific DSA test to gain Category D1) **and** Have passed an assessment test for this type of vehicle. Driving permits will be endorsed 'Personnel Carrier'. Cannot drive in emergency response mode using blue lights and sirens, or claim speed exemptions, unless also trained to standard response level with a current minimum driver training classification of 5.
PSU Personnel Carrier (Fully Protected - PSU Specification)	Use for PSU duty Fitted with blue lights and sirens. Will be marked (liveried). Vehicles classified within the "Specialist Vehicles" category "Authorised Only"	**1. PSU Duty - Trained Officers:** Driver must possess Category D1 on their DVLA driving licence. (Drivers who passed their DVSA driving test on or after 1/1/97 do not have the D1 category automatically included and must pass a specific DSA test to gain Category D1) **and** Have passed an assessment test for this type of vehicle and Will be at least standard response level with a current minimum driver permit classification of 5 Driving permits will be endorsed

Vehicle Type	Vehicle Use/Guidance	Driver Requirements
		'Personnel Carrier - PSU" **2. Non PSU Trained Officers / Non PSU duty:** Must have Category D1 on their DVLA driving licence (as above) **and** Have passed an assessment test for this type of vehicle. Driving permits will be endorsed 'Personnel Carrier'. Cannot drive in emergency response mode using blue lights and sirens, or claim speed exemptions, unless also trained to standard response level with a <u>current minimum</u> driver training classification of 5.
4 x 4 Utility (Non-RP) **Capable of Heavyweight Full Off-Road Cross Country Use.** {**NB:** For Lightweight off - road/green lane use see Response section above}.	Usually response vehicles, which are likely to be diesel eg, Mitsubishi Shogun 4 x4's (or future similar spec Vehicles). **Note:** It is recognised along with advancements in "Intelligent" vehicles electronics - 4X4's Fitted with blue lights and sirens. Vehicles will usually be marked (liveried). Suitable for response duties, use by Rural Crime teams etc. **Not** suitable for pursuits. Capable of heavyweight off-road use. Vehicle classification 5.	Driving permit minimum classification of 1 but To drive in emergency response role using blue lights and sirens, and be eligible to claim speed limit exemptions, drivers **must** be at least standard level with a current minimum driver training classification of 5.
DTU Vehicles	A range of vehicles, including motorcycles (or access to motorcycles) as necessary for driver/rider training purposes.	DTU Trainers must possess a current permit suitably reflecting the level required to both drive and instruct others in driving vehicles to

Vehicle Type	Vehicle Use/Guidance	Driver Requirements
	Can be marked or unmarked. Fitted with blue lights and sirens. May be 4x4 drive. For use for driver training. Vehicles classified within the "Specialist Vehicles" category "Authorised Only"	the standard and role required for the particular course, assessment or task. This may include the instruction or assessment of students in non DTU vehicles if required. Students themselves must possess the relevant DVLA driving licence category to drive the particular vehicle. The points above will be managed by the DTU Manager who will ensure that Instructor competencies are up to date. Operational commitments may dictate that other persons may, from time to time, be authorised by either the DTU Manager or, in an emergency by the FIM to drive a DTU vehicle - in which case they must drive within the limitations of their own driving permit. If an **operational** commitment (above) requires an emergency response (blue lights & sirens and eligibility to claim speed exemptions), a current driver permit level 5 will be required if the vehicle is response grade. If the DTU vehicle advanced the driver will require a current permit level 8.
Communications Vehicle **and** **(Combined) Exhibition Vehicle & Negotiators Vehicle - and future similar vehicles).**	Large vehicles which are unique and require no further identification. Vehicles classified within the "Specialist Vehicles" category "Authorised Only"	Driver must: Possess the appropriate DVLA driving licence for the particular vehicle (Fleet Mgr can advise on the specific requirement if advice required). Successfully undergo a Large Vehicle driving assessment with a DTU Instructor. Driving permits will be endorsed in the Authorised Specialist Vehicle Section with the appropriate vehicle specified vehicle on the permit.
Armoured Vehicle. (Currently a Mitsubishi Shogun 4 x4')	Advanced vehicle. Can be either marked or umarked vehicle. Fitted with blue lights & sirens For operational use only. including training by DTU.	Driver must: Possess the appropriate DVLA driving licence for the particular vehicle (Fleet Mgr can advise on the specific requirement if advice

Vehicle Type	Vehicle Use/Guidance	Driver Requirements
	A unique vehicle which requires no further identification. Will be marked **'Authorised Driver Only'**. Vehicles classified within "Specialist Vehicles" - 'Authorised Only'.	required). Be <u>advanced</u> level with a current minimum driver training classification of 8. Driving permits will be endorsed in the Authorised Specialist Vehicle Section with 'Armoured Vehicle'.
Firearms Incident Vehicles	Large, specially equipped vehicles which are unique and require no further identification. Marked or unmarked Fitted with blue lights and sirens Vehicles classified within "Specialist Vehicles" and will be marked 'Authorised Driver Only'.	Driver must: Be at least standard level with a current minimum driver training classification of 5. Possess the appropriate DVSA driving licence for the particular vehicle (Fleet Mgr can advise on the specific requirement if advice required). Be assessed by DTU as competent to drive these vehicles in their intended operational role. Driving permits will be endorsed in the Authorised Specialist Vehicle Section with **'Firearms Incident Vehicle'**.
Recovery Vehicle	Large vehicle which is unique and requires no further identification. Vehicles classified within the "Specialist Vehicles" category and will be marked 'Authorised Driver Only'.	Drivers must have the appropriate LGV driving licence. Driving permits will be endorsed in the Authorised Specialist Vehicle Section with **'Recovery Vehicle'**.
Vehicles Leased to Individual Staff	Applies to certain eligible staff whose position and/or role qualifies them to have the vehicle. May be response or advanced powered. Unmarked (non liveried). Dependent on the role, may be fitted with blue lights and sirens - although this will not apply to vehicles for police staff. Vehicles classified within the "Specialist Vehicles" category "Authorised Only"	Driving permits will be endorsed in the Authorised Specialist Vehicle Section with "Lease Vehicle" / have the appropriate vehicle specified vehicle on the permit. To drive in emergency response mode using blue lights and sirens, and be eligible to claim speed limit exemptions, (whether or not blue lights and sirens are in use) drivers **must** be at least Standard level with a <u>current</u> minimum driver training classification of 5. Drivers to note "Responding to Emergencies" section on page 50 of this procedure. The requirements of the Road Safety Act re speed exemptions will apply.

Vehicle Type	Vehicle Use/Guidance	Driver Requirements
Trailers	A limited number of trailers are used by the force. They may be braked or unbraked. Fleet manager is responsible for ensuring they are fit for the purpose required. Towbars are only fitted to certain vehicles identified and authorised by the Fleet Manager which are capable of towing trailers. Trailers are classified by the Fleet Manager within the "Specialist Vehicles" category. Further advice is available from Fleet Manager if required.	Driving permit minimum classification of 1. Drivers must ensure they possess the appropriate DSA driving licence category on their personal Driving Licence before they tow the trailer. (**If in any doubt** Fleet Mgr can advise on the specific requirement if advice required).

DRIVING PERMITS

Introduction

Driving permits are the means by which the Force manages who is eligible to drive which Police vehicles in the fleet and in what role.

The scheme assists the Force to manage occupational road risk by helping to ensure:
  ➢ we operate a safe system of work in relation to our on-road activities.
  ➢ every driver is aware of their particular authorisation level and any restrictions they must adhere to.
  ➢ our staff are competent and equipped to drive the vehicles provided for their particular role.

Requirements and Responsibility

1. All staff/Community Volunteers required to drive either police authority owned, hired, leased or loaned vehicles on force insurance as part of their employment or service to the organisation, no matter how infrequently, must first obtain a driving permit authorising them to drive at work.

    Police Staff and Community Volunteers may drive unmarked vehicles without partaking in a driver assessment but will have a full DVLA licence for the relevant category which will be presented, with the relevant form (Form 321), to the DTU prior to the issue of a driving permit. No member of staff or volunteer may drive police authority vehicles or for police purposes without being issued such a permit.

    However, staff/volunteers required to drive vans, personnel carriers and/or exhibition vehicles must undertake and successfully pass the relevant driving assessment. This is to ensure proven competence to safely drive such vehicles.

    The other exception to marked vehicles is the Community Volunteer vehicle which is marked specifically as such. All other members of police staff/ Officers must have undertaken and successfully passed the relevant driving assessment or course (as applicable), to ensure proven competence to safely drive vehicles for the particular purpose(s) required by their role. The final decision on whether an assessment is required for the relevant role will rest with the DTU manager and Head of Road Safety.

2. Both driving assessment and driver training course requirements need to be planned ahead and booked via RMU. A Driver Permit Application form can be found on Firstpoint under People Services / People Development /Driver Training.

3. Responsibility for ensuring driving permits remain current for staff required to hold standard response or advanced level permits, is a joint one and rests with Supervisors, RMU, Departmental Manager's - as well as the individual themselves. People Services will maintain records of driver training delivered and

update permit records, but they will not be responsible for issuing reminders for refresher training / assessments.

4. Shared responsibility is necessary to ensure this process is effectively managed and does not fail - so that where staff require either training or periodic driving assessments to perform their role, they undertake these assessments within specified timescales. **Future eligibility to claim legal exemptions from, for example, statutory speed limits in the course of their duties will depend on this.**

5. For standard emergency response and advanced drivers, current national guidance requires a refresher every 5 years. In practice, in some cases they may be conducted more frequently. If a refresher driving assessment is not successfully completed in accordance with this procedure, the individual's authorisation to perform that particular role will lapse.

6. An officer trained and authorised to either advanced or standard response driver/rider level, and who is deployed within a role where those training levels are neither used nor required, reverts to the level below after 12 months, ie, advanced reverts to standard response and standard response reverts to basic. This may follow a period of restricted duties or a posting to a role not requiring driving at either standard response or advanced level.

7. In certain circumstances, this procedure restricts the use to which a particular type of vehicle can be put by a particular category of driver. These restrictions are necessary to ensure the safety of everyone and in certain circumstances, comply with the law. They must be adhered to by all concerned.

8. Line management will decide at what level an individual driver's classification and authorisation needs to be and maintained at, in order to perform their role in accordance with this procedure. To manage training resources and abstraction of officers effectively, this decision will be based upon organisational need - not simply the wish of a particular individual.

Driving Permit Record

There is no requirement for staff to carry driving permits.

Electronic permits in microsoft word or other appropriate software format will be issued by People Services. They are the authorised SPOC responsible for issuing and maintaining all new, replacement or amended driver permit records. No-one else will alter or amend driving permits. People Services will e mail a copy to the member of staff concerned, but there will be no need for anyone to routinely print them off. New permits will not be issued retrospectively.

If under this procedure circumstances arise where an individual's permit requires amendment, the Dept concerned, (or in the case of the awarding of permit penalty points (see "Penalty Points" page 41), the Force Operations Department must request People Services to amend the permit accordingly and provide details of the amendment to them via e mail).

People Services will ensure:

> ➢ accurate, up-to-date permit records exist for authorised drivers
> ➢ individuals are notified by e-mail of any changes to their driving permit. They will be given sight of the permit whenever changes occur and requested to agree it is correct.
> ➢ any unresolved dispute over accuracy or unresolved query will be referred to a DTU Manager if it relates to authorisation level or driving assessments, or to the Force Operations Department if it relates to penalty points awarded or any other issue.
> ➢ sight of any driving permit is given (usually via e-mail attachment) to any member of staff/volunteer of supervisory rank or position, having reasonable grounds to see it.
> ➢ following a request, any officer, Community Volunteer or member of police staff may see their permit at any reasonable time.

Posting or Transfer of Staff

- Upon being posted or transferred to a different department or role, the member of staff and their supervisor will liaise regarding that individual's current driver permit status. This is particularly important if the permit held is either standard response or advanced level and they require, or are likely to require, regular driving assessments in accordance with this procedure to perform their operational role.

- The supervisor may if needed, access a copy of the permit. If a high speed driving permit is not required for the officers new role the new supervisor should inform DTU so an updated permit can be issued.

- The new supervisor will ensure, in consultation with line management, that if the individual is likely to require future driving assessments to maintain their current driver classification, both RMU and any designated person in their department responsible for forward planning of driver assessments, is made aware of the date the next driving assessment must be completed by. The appropriate action must then be taken to ensure the next assessment is progressed in a timely fashion, ie within 5 years of the previous driving course or assessment - whichever is applicable.

Format of Driving Permits

Driving Permits will be of a format and design prescribed by the DTU Manager. Their format will be adapted as necessary to suit current policing and DTU requirements. The permit record will however contain the following information:

> The individual's name (rank if appropriate) and Force number (if applicable)
> The vehicle classifications the individual is authorised to drive
> The level of driver training received
> Any authorised specialist vehicle categories the individual is entitled to drive
> The nature of any restrictions imposed
> The number of penalty points accumulated within the last 3 years and
> The permit expiry date

Shelf Life: Driver Training & Permit Classifications and Authorisations

NB: Tables summarising the relationship between driver training levels, vehicle classifications and individual roles can be viewed between pages 10 and 13. The detailed table starting on page 14 covers practical application and is a reference point for all staff.

1. "Shelf life" of driver permits is dependent upon both the operational level and current role of the driver, set against corresponding national competencies, driver training requirements and guidance, including any relevant DSA requirements. These are subject to change.
   The individual demands placed upon our drivers and the inherent risks within those demands will vary. The "shelf life" is a necessary control measure to help manage this proportionately, responsibly and effectively.

2. Current national recommendations require that "a return to driving duties, after 12 months or more absence from a particular standard, should be accompanied by an appropriate assessment and refresher training provided as necessary". In practice this will apply to both standard and advanced level drivers.

3. Examples of normal refresher timescales would include:

Standard Response Driving	5 Years
Response Motorcycling	2 Years
Advanced Driving	5 Years
Initial Phase Pursuit (IPP)	5 Years
Tactical Phase Pursuit (TPAC)	3 Years
VIP Protection Driving/Riding	2 Years
Pursuit for Comms/Supervisors	3 Years
Pre-surveillance Motorcycle Riding	2 Years

Advice on an individual basis can be obtained from the DTU.

Classification 1 Police Staff – Volunteer (grey fleet/marked volunteer car) – NO ASSESSMENT

Usually valid for the duration of the individual's affiliation with the force. This takes into account the fact the individual will maintain their skills on a daily basis and that no higher level of driving is required than that of DSA test standard.

This category takes account of volunteers now working within the organisation and also falling in line with the Police Driving APP whereby it is ackowledged that not all roles involving driving require an assessment. The fact that they hold a current UK driving licence is satisfactory for this classification.

Staff required to drive vans, personel carriers or exhibition vehicles must have undertaken and successfully passed the relevant driving assessment. This is to ensure proven competence to safely drive such vehicles.

Supervisors/Line Managers must ensure that staff/volunteers are conversant with fuelling requirements and daily vehicle checks to ensure that fleet vehicles are always ready for use.

Classification 2: PCSO – Police Basic Assessment

Usually remain valid for the duration of the individual's employment with the force. This takes into account the fact the individual will maintain their skills on a daily basis and that no higher level of driving is required than that of DSA test standard.

Classification 3: Police Basic

Usually remain valid for the duration of the individual's employment with the force. This takes into account the fact the individual will maintain their skills on a daily basis and that no higher level of driving is required than that of DSA test standard.

Classification 4: Police Basic - Authorised to Stop Vehicles

The only difference between this classification and classification 3 is that drivers will have received formal training in the safe stopping of vehicles on the public highway. This authorisation will also usually remain valid for the duration of the individual's employment with the force.

Classifications 5 and 6: Standard Response and Standard Response (Hostyds Trained)

The only difference between classifications 5 and 6 is that drivers classified as 6 will have received Hostyds training / assessment as part of a Standard Driving/Initial Pursuit Course (& any subsequent Initial Pursuit assessments or training.

Authorisation level will remain valid for a period not exceeding 5 years. A successful standard driving refresher conducted by the DTU, is required between 3 to 5 years to maintain permit validity. The driver's permit will otherwise be considered to have expired and their permit authorisation will automatically be reduced to level 4 'Police Basic - Stop Vehicles'.

If operational need exists and it is authorised, (see "Requests for Driver Training" pages 33/34), the driver can regain his previous permit level upon successfully passing either a standard driving refresher or standard driving course, whichever is deemed necessary by the DTU at the time in the particular circumstances.

Classification 7:

Not Currently Used.

Classifications 8 and 9: Advanced Car and TPAC

The only difference between classifications 8 and 9 is that drivers classified as 9 will be TPAC trained. Only drivers currently posted to Specialist Ops or DCT will receive TPAC training/refreshers and be in suitable vehicles. The latter issue (suitable vehicles), always needs to be considered as part of any DRA for TPAC deployment.

Authorisation level will remain valid for a period not exceeding 5 years. A successful advanced driving assessment, conducted by the DTU, is required every 5 years to maintain permit validity for classification 8. To retain permit validity for classification 9, drivers must pass both an advanced assessment and a TPAC refresher course or assessment - whichever applies at the time - within the 3 year period. The driver's permit will otherwise be considered to have expired for the particular classification.

If the driver's permit expires their permit authorisation will automatically be reduced as follows:

- From classification 9 to 8 - if an advanced driving assessment is passed without TPAC
- From classification 9 or 8 to level 5 if an advanced driving assessment is not passed within the 5 year period.

If there is operational need and it is authorised, (see section on "Requests for Driver Training" page 37), a driver can regain their previous permit level upon successfully passing either an advanced driving assessment and/or a TPAC refresher course or assessment, whichever of these is deemed necessary by the DTU at the time, in the particular circumstances.

The DTU Manager may implement TPAC refresher training or assessments more frequently if he/she considers it necessary and would do so in discussion with Specialist Ops.

Classification "Authorised Only"

This permit classification includes authorisation to drive or ride one or more types of vehicle which themselves are classified as "Authorised Only." This can include vehicles attracting particular legal requirements in so far as driver licensing is concerned, eg, Personnel Carrier. In each case, the individual characteristics of these vehicles together with their role have been considered jointly by the Driver Training Manager and Fleet Manager, before coming to a decision about the appropriate driver permit level and the need/frequency of driving assessment. Individual permits will contain more detail. Further advice can be obtained from either the Fleet or DTU Managers as appropriate.

DRIVER TRAINING/ASSESSMENT

Overview

Force Driver Training Strategy ensures all drivers are trained and authorised to nationally agreed competencies and occupational standards - and in accordance with any associated legislation, code of practice and NPCC/ APP guidance where these apply. Approved training course content will be complied with, together with any relevant DSA requirements.

This procedure is not intended to cover detailed day to day DTU standard operating procedures, but the following points and guidance will be helpful.

All driving courses and driving assessments will be conducted by appropriately qualified staff from the DTU.

A driving instructor from another force may be used if the need arises - this will be at the discretion of the DTU Manager, according to organisational need at the time.

Driving Courses/Assessments

A full list of driving courses and prospectuses may be viewed on Firstpoint under People Services/People Development /Driver Training.

Staff who require either training or periodic driving assessments to perform their role, must undertake these within specified timescales. **Future eligibility to claim legal exemptions from, for example, statutory speed limits in the course of their duties will depend on this.**

For standard emergency response and advanced drivers, current national guidance requires a refresher every 5 years. In practice, in some cases they may be conducted more frequently.

Requests for Driver Training

NB: The 1st bullet point below is extracted from the "Driver Permits" section of this procedure for ease of reference.

- Line management will decide at what level an individual's driver's classification and authorisation needs to be and maintained at, in order to perform their role in accordance this procedure. To manage training resources and abstraction of officers effectively, this decision will be based upon organisational need - not simply the wish of a particular individual.

- To put a member of staff through a standard response or advanced driving course is a significant commitment for the DTU and requires significant abstraction time for the individual away from their day to day role.

- Resource constraints and the pressing need to prioritise driver training to meet essential operational requirements, as well as compulsory standard emergency response and advanced driver national competencies, require that requests for both standard and advanced driver courses, will have been authorised by an officer not below the rank of Inspector.

- If advice is needed, line managers are encouraged to contact the DTU.

Referral for Driving Assessment - Supervisors Recommendation

- Whilst the bulk of police supervisors may not have any particular aptitude or skill as driver trainers, as police officers they are expected to be capable of identifying poor driving. Where an individual's standard of driving of a police vehicle, or apparent cavalier attitude, causes a supervisor particular concern, the supervisor may if they consider it prudent, recommend to the Force Operations Department that the member of staff concerned be given a driving assessment by the DTU. This recommendation will be made and evidenced by way of a report, which will outline briefly the circumstances that have led to the concern.

- There must be a presumption that supervisors submitting a recommendation under this section will be supported. It is recognised the decision to submit such a report will not be made lightly and there will be a presumption in favour of individual and public safety. It is recognised concern or perceived criticisms about an individual's driving can be contentious and taken "personally" by the individual. Whilst being aware of that fact, everyone involved has a responsibility to recognise that as an emergency service employer, public expectation is that the standard of driving from our employees whilst driving police vehicles, will be exemplary and, above all, safe. The onus should be placed upon the DTU to resolve any concerns, whereby a professionally trained police driving instructor conducts a driving assessment to discharge the duty of care owed in these circumstances.

- Where concern arises following involvement in a police vehicle road traffic collision, the Force Operations Department will in accordance with this procedure, review previous such incidents in force involving the individual and determine whether in the individual circumstances, remedial driving measures are appropriate - consulting as necessary with the DTU Manager. The need for a driving assessment will be considered as part of this process. (See "Remedial Action - Drivers" page 36).

Transferees - Driving Assessment

The level of assessment will be based upon organisational need regarding their new role in this force. Transferee Police Officers or staff qualified from other Force assessments will be reviewed by DTU as to their suitability to drive operational vehicles in the role and context they are now in.

Managers and RMU have a responsibility to arrange driving assessments as soon as practicable to comply with this procedure. If drivers need to be eligible to claim speed exemptions as part of their role - it is essential there is no delay as this could affect their eligibility to do so under the provisions of the Road Safety Act.

Standard Drivers:

- If the officer is to be posted to Response Duties or another post which demands eligibility to claim speed exemptions, there is clear benefit to the organisation in retaining current standard driving skills where they possess them. Officers coming into force who possessed a **current** standard driver permit in their previous force (enabling emergency response driving), do not require an assessment from the DTU - provided the officer has actually regularly performed a response driver role within the previous 12 months and can evidence this. (However see the following three bullet points).

- A gap of more than 12 months **will** trigger the requirement for a refresher before a standard response level permit can be issued.

- The officer's next refresher must take place within 5 years of their previous assessment in any event. Therefore if the officer has not had either a driving refresher or a standard driver training course within the previous 5 years, then regardless of the above, they must undertake a refresher with the DTU, before being issued with a standard driver permit.

- Irrespective of the above, consideration must include standard refresher training by the DTU to ensure force policy is complied with regarding force (initial) Pursuit procedures. If they are posted to response duties, they need to be Initial Pursuit Trained.

- If advice is needed, line managers are encouraged to contact the DTU.

Advanced Drivers:

- If the officer is to be posted to a role requiring an advanced permit, a similar policy to that of standard drivers will be adopted in respect of officers who previously held advanced driver permits, whether TPAC trained or not. They must have performed operational RPU/AFO duties in their previous force as an advanced driver within the previous 12 months and have had a driving assessment or an advanced course within the previous 5 years.

- If they are posted to Roads Policing, they will need to be TPAC trained if they are not. In considering requirements, care will be needed if TPAC Training/Tactics in their previous force were different to Specialist Operations.

- If they are an advanced driver and posted to Uniform Response Duties, or elsewhere with no early likelihood of being posted to a role requiring an advanced permit, they will undergo a driving refresher to standard level if/when a refresher is required under this procedure.

Basic Level Drivers

- Volunteers and members of staff who are ex police trained drivers (standard or advanced within last 12 months), and who require basic driver classification for their role, may be issued with a basic permit without the need for an assessment.

- In all other cases the officer or member of police staff will undergo a basic driving assessment commensurate with the requirements of their new role.

Driving Licence, Eyesight Test and Relevant Knowledge - Requirement

Prior to the commencement of any driving assessment or driving course all students will

Produce their driving licence at the DTU for inspection.

Undergo an eyesight test. For standard response drivers and above, this test will comply with the Group 2 Medical Standard as published by the DVLA, or any such standard that may replace it in future.

Be expected to be conversant with the Highway Code and force driving procedure as it applies to them and their role.

Undertake and pass a relevant knowledge test or examination, if applicable.

DTU Procedure: General Information

Driver training authorisation procedure is divided into two parts - theory and practical assessment. Candidates are required to successfully complete both parts of this process prior to being authorised to drive force vehicles of the classification their role requires.

Upon successful completion of the driving course or assessment, authorisation will be confirmed by the DTU to the student and DTU will ensure People Services are notified.

Where a member of staff fails their driver training course or assessment, the DTU will be responsible for identifying and advising on further individual training needs. Liaison as necessary will take place between DTU and line management to progress this before the member of staff undergoes further assessment. In some cases, DTU may conclude the particular member of staff does not currently possess the potential or ability to pass the required course or assessment level.

Further detailed DTU operating procedures not covered within the scope of this procedure, will reflect current national and force / Specialist Operations requirements.

REMEDIAL ACTION - DRIVERS

1   Introduction

1.1   As an emergency service employer, the force must manage its obligations in relation to occupational road risk and health and safety effectively. This must be proportionate to the risks involved to properly discharge the force's duty of care to its employees and the public. Immediate response driving using blue lights and sirens attracts a high level of risk, which is why the police service requires both standard response and advanced drivers to be trained and periodically refreshed to meet national training competencies and standards. When something "goes wrong" or is alleged to have "gone wrong", there is a need to ensure remedial measures are actioned which:

- are reasonable and proportionate to both the occurrence and level of risk,
- take into account the individual's current authorised driver classification, driving history and the driving demands of their current role,
- consistent in their application and,
- in the case of trained police drivers (standard response or advanced level), they meet

  - ➢ any legal requirements and/or code of practice
  - ➢ current national police driver training standards and
  - ➢ any accompanying NPCC APP or other guidance.

In practice this means all driver training or assessments must be delivered by an authorised driving instructor from the DTU. Where necessary, a force driving instructor from another force may be used if the need arises - this will be at the discretion of the DTU Manager according to organisational need at the time.

1.2   The implementation of this procedure does not affect the position of the Force in those circumstances where a police vehicle is used in such a manner that may contravene the law.

1.3   The allocation of internal penalty points on driver permits will not be used as an alternative to prosecution. Remedial action such as driving suspension, other restrictions, or driver training / assessment, does not seek to prejudge any investigation or prosecution outcome, but should be viewed as exercising the duty of care the force owe to both its staff and the public we serve, as part of a robust approach to responsibly managing occupational road risk.

1.4   Where offence proceedings are being considered, the process of allocating penalty points (section 4 below) will be suspended until such time as a final decision regarding prosecution is made.

2   Remedial Action

2.1   It is necessary for clarity and effective management, to draw a distinction between:

- incidents occurring when driving in immediate response mode with blue lights and/or sirens, and,

- incidents which do not, (whether on or off duty - and whether in a police vehicle or private vehicle), and,
- the action that should be taken in each scenario - always accepting the individual circumstances will be a consideration.

2.2 To ensure consistency of application and continuity, the Force Operations Inspector is the designated post in force for consideration of driving related remedial action in each case. In appropriate cases, pending remedial action, he/she will consider suspension of the driver from driving or restrict their driver permit (for example to <u>non</u> immediate response driving), as a necessary control measure. This will not prevent another supervisor or manager from suspending a driver from driving police vehicles until such time as the Force Operations Inspector has reviewed the matter and made his/her decision.

2.3 The advice of the DTU Manager should be sought prior to any decision regarding further driver training or standard response/advanced driving assessment.

2.4 From time to time, the very high standards required of emergency response and advanced drivers may, in particular individual circumstances, mean an individual driver is not considered suitable to return to immediate response driving.

Rationale

2.5 The demands on, and expectations of, professionally trained standard response and advanced level police drivers attract national training and assessment competencies commensurate with the roles they are expected to perform. Whilst performing those roles, police drivers must at all times meet the standards required of them. These attract a higher level of demands, different professional application of training and "mindset" to that required when not driving in emergency response mode - when the demands and standards (DSA as opposed to Police), are lower.

Effective occupational road risk and health and safety management must meet the requirements in the workplace, but cannot ignore reported incidents occurring outside the workplace "off duty". It is contended this procedure strikes a proportionate balance in all the scenarios below.

<u>Nothing within this procedure shall prevent further measures being implemented or reviewed in accordance with this procedure if considered necessary in the particular individual circumstances at any time</u>, for example a driver permit suspension - as opposed to a restriction not to drive in immediate response mode.

On Duty Incidents - Immediate Response:

<u>Police Vehicle Collision - (Injury or Non Injury):</u>

2.6 If the police driver is clearly at fault, or may be at fault, ie their driving could be considered to be careless (section 3 road traffic act), then pending either any decision by CPS on prosecution or subsequent court proceedings, the driver will not be permitted to drive in immediate response mode or pursue any vehicle that has failed to stop, until the case has been disposed of. <u>In addition</u>, the driver must undergo a standard or advanced driving refresher course, (whichever is appropriate to the individual's role). However see paragraph 2.8 below.

2.7 If at an early stage, the manner of driving is considered to be more serious - such that it could well amount to dangerous driving (section 2 Road Traffic Act) as opposed to the lesser offence of careless driving, then restrictions per 2.6 above will be imposed, but consideration will be given to the driver undergoing a full standard or advanced driving course (whichever is appropriate to the individual's role) - as opposed to a shorter refresher course.

2.8 If a decision is made by CPS to prosecute the police driver, under section 2 or 3 of the Road Traffic Act, the Force Operations Inspector or most appropriate manager of the relevant department must be notified and he/she will review the matter further in consultation with the DTU Manager. The option of requiring the driver to attend a full driving course at the appropriate level will be a consideration if not (eg in section 2 cases) already imposed, but the decision will be in the context of considering the individual circumstances - including (for careless driving cases) - whether or not the driver has since attended and passed a refresher course.

2.9 If the driver is convicted at court of either careless or dangerous driving (section 2 or 3 Road Traffic Act), the Force Operations Inspector, as well as PSD must be notified. He/she will review the matter further, in consultation with the DTU Manager, to consider and determine whether in the individual circumstances, any further remedial driving measures are necessary. Account will be taken of remedial action implemented in the interim period and any other relevant information and considerations to hand since.

Allegation Careless or Dangerous Driving (Immediate Response/Non RTC):

2.10 Will be dealt with broadly in line with the above. The "trigger point" for consideration of remedial driving measures, will be where it is deemed there is sufficient evidence for a notice of intended prosecution (NOIP) to be sent to the police driver. Justice Traffic must therefore inform the Force Operations Inspector that a NOIP has been sent and ensure he/she has sufficient information to review the matter at an early stage, to make a decision as to appropriate restrictions / remedial measures in the individual circumstances.

(As per 2.3 above and if applicable in the particular circumstances, the Force Operations Inspector will seek the advice of the DTU Manager prior to any decision regarding further driver training or standard response/advanced driving assessment).

2.11 If, having served the NOIP, a decision is subsequently taken by either Justice Traffic or CPS, that the available evidence is not sufficient to support a prosecution, the Force Operations Inspector will be informed. He/she will review the matter again to determine any further remedial action required in the circumstances.

On Duty Incidents - Not Immediate Response:

Police Vehicle Collision Occurs - (Injury or Non Injury):

2.12 NB: This section would apply to basic level trained drivers as well.
If the police driver is clearly at fault, or could be at fault, they may be required to undergo a formal driving assessment that meets the current national standard for their particular training level (ie basic, standard or advanced).

Note: The above is not intended to apply to minor, damage only collisions that occur for example, when manoeuvring, or on private/police property for example. However such incidents will still attract due consideration of internal penalty points on driving permits by the Force Operations Department - and any further remedial action emanating from the driver's history in that regard.

It should be noted that whatever the circumstances are that the police driver is expected to wait at the scene and call for a local supervisor to attend and deal with the POLACC. The supervisor will ensure that all procedures required by the road traffic act are carried out and see that the welfare of those involved is taken care of.

Allegation Careless or Dangerous Driving (Non RTC - Immediate Response):

2.13 Will be dealt with broadly in line with 2.12 above. The "trigger point" for consideration of remedial driving measures, will be where it is deemed that there is sufficient evidence for a notice of intended prosecution (NOIP) to be sent to the police driver. Justice Traffic must therefore inform the Force Operations Inspector that a NOIP has been sent and ensure he/she has sufficient information to review the matter at an early stage, to make a decision as to restrictions/remedial measures in the individual circumstances.

2.14 If, having served the NOIP, a decision is subsequently taken by either Justice Traffic or CPS, that the available evidence is not sufficient to support a prosecution, the Force Operations Inspector will be informed and he/she will review the matter again to determine any further remedial action required in the circumstances.

Off Duty Incidents:

2.15 **Note:** This procedure includes a separate section on "Employees Obligations" which requires both police officers and police staff to report certain offences to PSD on any occasion in the UK or elsewhere, when they have been either served with a summons, issued with a fixed penalty notice for a road traffic offence, charged, cautioned, convicted, sentenced, or given conditions imposed by any court. This would include for example, cases of careless or dangerous driving. This makes clear the above relates to driving either police authority or privately owned vehicles.

2.16 Under this new section of the procedure it will now be incumbent on PSD to inform the Force Operations Inspector of the circumstances reported ASAP, to enable him/her to review the matter and make a decision as to the imposition of any necessary driving restrictions/remedial measures in the individual circumstances, in accordance with paragraphs 2.17 & 2.18 below.

2.17 If the driver has received a summons for careless driving, <u>or</u>
is charged, cautioned, or convicted of that offence <u>and</u>
they are a current basic, standard or advanced driver

the expectation is that the driver will be referred to the DTU for a formal driving assessment. If the offence is dangerous driving, the expectation is that the driver will undergo a standard driving refresher course or, in the case of an advanced driver, an advanced refresher driving course. If a NOIP has been served on the driver and Justice Traffic are aware, (i.e. the offence took place in Force area), they must inform the Force Operations Inspector and ensure he/she has sufficient information to review the matter at an early stage, to make a decision as to restrictions/remedial measures in the individual circumstances. If the driver's permit level is basic (either police officer, or police staff), ie they are **not** police trained - the driver will undergo a basic level driving assessment test. This takes into account that no higher level of driving is required of them at work than that of the DSA test standard.

2.18 If an off duty RTC/Incident involving a standard/advanced trained driver is deemed suitable for an NDORS Driver Improvement Scheme Course (NDORS DIS), then in addition to that (public) disposal, the driver will also attend the DTU for a standard or advanced level assessment. This will ensure occupational road risk is managed effectively and takes account of the fact that NDORS DIS is not designed to cater for emergency service drivers and is set at the lower (DSA) level of driving, whilst at the same time recognising that NDORS DIS is an alternative to a Section 3 RTA prosecution for careless driving.

3. Options List: Remedial Action - Drivers

3.1 The options below are not new. They exist to help the Force Operations Department and in appropriate cases, line management, decide on the action/intervention necessary in particular individual circumstances. They are applicable to the scenarios above and to the application of the driver permit "Penalty Points System" (see next section of this procedure).

3.2 The Force Operations Department will select a course of action from the list set out below. Where non-driving related options are under consideration, e.g., posting or discipline, this will be managed by the driver's line management, in conjunction as appropriate with PSD.

3.3 In some cases it may be appropriate to combine two or more options. It is reiterated the advice of the DTU Manager should be sought prior to any decision regarding further driver training or standard response / advanced assessment.

3.4 If circumstances arise where an individual's permit requires amendment, the Force Operations Department will request the People Services to amend the permit accordingly and those details must be provided in writing.

OPTION	CIRCUMSTANCES
No Action at this time	No further action need be taken at this time, having regard to all of the circumstances.
Driving Permit Restriction	Restrictions on the manner or circumstances in which the driver may drive police vehicles may be imposed.
Driving Suspension	The driver will be suspended from driving police vehicles. The suspension may relate to all vehicles or specific classes of vehicles. The period of driving suspension will be specified.
Driving Assessment	The driver will be required to undertake a driving assessment in accordance with their driver training level. Where a driver fails to reach the appropriate standard, remedial training should be considered in the first instance, in conjunction with the DTU.
Training (Driving Course)	The driver will be required to undertake a course of instruction to the particular operational standard required (standard or advanced). There may in practice be occasions where the appropriate starting point will be a driving assessment. In such cases it is stressed that the advice of the DTU Manager should be sought.
Driving Permit Classification Amendment	The performance classification of vehicles that the staff member is authorised to drive may be reduced.
Advice	The member of staff will be advised either verbally or in writing - in relation to their driver history and future conduct. This advice will be recorded on the staff member's personal file.
Penalty Points on Permit	See Penalty Points Procedure below.
Posting	1. In the particular individual circumstances, Line Management may decide the driver should be posted to another location or role until an investigation and any prosecution and/or discipline considerations are dealt with. 2. Taking account of the driver's history, he/she may be transferred to an operational / non operational environment where the driving requirements are more suited to their skill level.
Discipline	Nothing within these proposals prevents the Force Operations Department, or the driver's Line Management/any other Supervisor from instigating disciplinary proceedings arising from the operation of police vehicles.

3.5   In line with paragraph 3.2 above the Force Operations Department will ensure that appropriate liaison with the driver's Line Management takes place as required.

3.6   **Driving Suspension:** It is reiterated nothing within this procedure will prevent the driver being suspended from driving police vehicles, if considered necessary in the particular individual circumstances at any time.

4.   Penalty Points Procedure - Driving Permits

4.1   The internal driving permit points procedure was designed to assist in the effective management of the vehicle fleet. It is reiterated:

- The implementation of this procedure does not affect the position of the Force in those circumstances where a police vehicle is used in such a manner that may contravene the law.

- The allocation of internal penalty points will not be used as an alternative to either prosecution or remedial measures. Action such as driving suspension or restrictions - or remedial measures such as driver training / assessment, does not seek to prejudge any investigation or prosecution outcome, but must be viewed as exercising the duty of care the force owe to both its staff and the public we serve, as part of a robust approach to responsibly managing occupational road risk as an emergency service.

Allocation of Points:

4.2 In circumstances where a police vehicle is used below the standard reasonably expected, then having regard to all of the circumstances, the Force Operations Department may impose points on a driver's permit.

4.3 The points are an indication of the driver's history and are not in themselves a punishment, or a sanction.

4.4 The Force Operations Department will review all such incidents in force and will determine reasonable use and the allocation of points on the driver's permit.

4.5 The number of points allocated as a consequence of a particular incident will reflect the extent to which the vehicle's use was considered unreasonable.

4.6 In coming to a decision, due consideration should be given alongside this, to any perceived need for a driving assessment and/or course of instruction for the individual concerned. This must be a subjective and proportionate decision, based upon the individual circumstances. It would by no means be expected to be necessary in each and every case. The advice of the DTU Manager should be sought prior to any decision regarding either further driver training or assessment.

4.7 Points will be allocated from one category of the table set out below per incident.

DRIVING INCIDENT	DRIVER PERMIT POINTS
Poor Driving	1 - 10
Unauthorised use of vehicle	3 - 10
Vehicle used as an inappropriate obstruction	3 - 10
Poor assessment of hazard	3 - 10
Pursuits - inappropriate	3 - 10
Excess speed for circumstances	1 - 6
Overtaking	3 - 6
Following too close (minor damage)	2 - 5.
Driving off road	2 - 5.
Grounding vehicle	2 - 5.
Poor nearside, offside judgement	1 - 3
Reversing	1 - 3

4.8 When points are allocated by the Force Operations Department, Justice Traffic will be informed of the decision, record it and notify People Services who will suitably endorse the driving permit.

Action When Driver Accrues 6 or more Points within 3 years:

4.9 To aide effective management of occupational road risk, a control measure is in place whereby, any member of staff who accrues 6 or more points within a 3 year period, will have their driving history with the force reviewed. The Force Operations Department will carry out the review and initiate appropriate action (in effect an Action Plan) to address any issues/concerns arising.

4.10 People Services will notify the Force Operations Department and DTU Manager when a permit holder has acquired 6 or more points within 3 years to trigger the review/action process required.

4.11 The decision on appropriate action will take into account the individual's current authorised driver classification, permit level and the driving demands of their current role.

- If the driver's role has attracted police driver training and consequently they possess a standard response permit or above, the Force Operations Department will instigate appropriate remedial action as set out in paragraphs 4.1 to 4.6 above.

- However where the driver's role requires a basic driving assessment to a standard no higher than that required of DSA test standard, the Force Operations Department will consider an appropriate action plan in liaison with that individual's line manager and recommend accordingly. This may include one or more of the disposals from the option list underneath para 4.4 above as considered proportionate and necessary in the circumstances.

4.12 Where a member of staff subsequently fails a driving assessment or course, the DTU will be responsible for identifying and advising on any further individual training needs. (See "DTU Procedure General Information" under "Driver Training" in this procedure).

4.13 Where the individual subsequently fails to achieve the action plan, and it is considered a point has been reached where, despite further reasonable assistance/attempts they can't achieve it, then in the absence of a more appropriate measure, line management will invoke Unsatisfactory Procedures as considered appropriate in the particular circumstances.

Totting Up (Permit) Penalty Points

4.14 When a police driver accrues 12 points on their driving permit, they will be immediately removed from driving in immediate response mode or engaging in any form of pursuit. They will return to 'Basic' level driving status. As soon as their points total falls below 12, they will be eligible for a full driving course subject to availability, line management approval and organisational requirements.

The Force Operations Department will consider the matter in liaison with others accordingly. The advice of the DTU Manager should be sought prior to any decision.

4.15 Permit points are effective (live) on a permit for a period of three years, therefore if the first points were accrued 2 .5 years prior to the driver reaching 12, then the 12 point rule above will only apply for the following six months.

Offence Proceedings

NB: If the matter concerns speeding and/or red light offences involving vehicles apparently being driven in immediate response mode with or without blue lights displayed, then in addition to the procedure below, paragraph 4.20 in particular should be noted and observed.

4.16 In circumstances where offence proceedings are being considered, the process of allocating points will be suspended until such time as a final decision as to prosecution is made. Either the Force Operations Department or Line Management may restrict the driving duties of a member of staff during this period, where they consider it is in the interest of the force and/or the individual, to do so.

4.17 Where an offence of excess speed or failure to conform to red traffic lights is detected by either a remote fixed site or mobile safety camera, a Notice of Intended Prosecution (NOIP) will be generated.

4.18 This will be sent to the Vehicle Fleet Manager who will identify the Department responsible for the vehicle and forward it to them.

4.19 Enquiries will be made to identify the driver and reasons for the offence. If applicable, an application for exemption **(form 162 templates)** will be completed. This will be signed by the Department Head or an Inspector or above and the documents forwarded to the Force Operations Department for a decision on whether to take no further action or continue process. The forms and any papers will then be returned to the originator. Senior Officers should follow their chain of command to authorise an exemption prior to it being sent to the Force Operations Department.

4.20 Whenever a driver is prosecuted in a court and found 'not guilty', the Force Operations Inspector will review the incident and consider the allocation of points, etc.

4.21 Where a decision not to prosecute is arrived at, the action as at 4.20 will apply.

4.22 The following procedure takes account of changes to published ACPO procedure with effect from 31/08/2007 - which deals with the way in which police and other emergency service vehicles can be exempted from camera detected red light and speed offences.

- This provision applies to all police vehicles being driven in an emergency response capacity.

- If a police vehicle activates a safety camera due to excess speed or travelling through a red light and it is obvious from the still picture taken by the camera, blue lights were in use, the relevant Safety Camera Unit will exempt the offence on behalf of the police driver.

- To reduce the administrative process, STORM logs can be tagged to indicate a marked/unmarked Police vehicle was being used at the time for prescribed police purposes and, that observing the speed limit or red light would have hindered the use of the vehicle for the purpose for which it was being used on that occasion.

- Where staff responding to an incident in any Police vehicle using blue lights, activate a speed or red light safety camera, they will contact the ECC for the STORM log to be tagged.

The information that the ECC requires is:

- The driver's force identification number.

- The precise location of the activation (includes direction of travel where cameras are positioned on both sides of a road).

- The registration number and/or fleet number of the police vehicle being driven.

- If no blue lights are visible and no corresponding "tagged" STORM log can be located by the relevant Camera Safety Unit, a Form 172 / NOIP will be issued in the normal way and the formal exemption process will need to be carried out.

Incidents involving personnel/vehicles from other forces

4.23 This 'points' procedure will not be used for driving incidents involving officers or vehicles from other forces. It will, however, be applicable to our staff whilst driving a police vehicle outside our force area.

Appeals

4.24 Where any member of staff feels aggrieved at the allocation of permit points, or the remedial action taken, they may appeal. The appeal will be in writing on form 232, setting out specifically the nature and grounds of their complaint.

4.25 The report will be submitted to their Superintendent and copied to the Force Operations Inspector.

4.26 The Superintendent will be responsible for dealing with the appeal. In every case, having considered the facts, they will send their written decision to the member of staff and copy to the Force Operations Inspector. The decision regarding the way in which the appeal will be dealt with will be made by the Superintendent. In cases where it is not possible to resolve the appeal, the matter will be referred to the Assistant Chief Constable for a final ruling.

4.27 The procedure above is available in addition to the force Issues Resolution Procedure.

Expired (Permit) Points

4.28 Drivers may request People Services to expunge expired points accrued over the previous three years from their permit. They must specify in writing (e mail) the changes necessary to their permit. People Services will retain a copy of each request for audit trail purposes. Any query over a particular request may be referred to the Force Operations Department.

MISCELLANEOUS PROVISIONS

Adverse Weather Conditions

Staff have an individual responsibility to drive according to the prevailing conditions.
Where road or weather conditions are such that continued driving is unwise or unsafe, drivers should seek the advice of a supervisory officer as to whether a journey or routine patrol should continue. Officers will consult as necessary with the duty CIM/FIM via ECC for further advice, or their duty Inspector.

The force have a number of 4x4 vehicles in the fleet and in severe adverse weather conditions these will be deployed to help maintain general operational resilience. This will include 4X4 ARV's driven by Tri Force Specialist Operations, unless a particular incident or threat dictates otherwise.

The force and its partners will activate contingency measures as necessary as part of emergency planning procedures.

Carriage of Passengers

- A Police vehicle can only be used for police purposes. It is not a taxi.
- Only persons engaged in police related duties or matters connected there-with, are permitted to use, ride in or on, any police vehicle.
- Except in an emergency, the carriage of civilian passengers outside of the above must be authorised by a Supervisor.

Parking Police and Private Vehicles for Police Purposes in "No Waiting Areas" (also reinforced in APP)

Vehicles will only be parked in a "no waiting" area in cases of operational necessity or where a space has been specifically reserved and marked for police vehicles.

Where a vehicle has been parked in such an area and the driver subsequently finds there is no longer a justifiable necessity for the vehicle to remain there, the vehicle will be moved asap.

Staff on routine enquiries will not contravene "no waiting" restrictions. Local parking regulations and the law will be observed and a good example set in terms of local policing. Local council enforcement staff and members of the public do not expect to see staff parked on double yellow lines when there is no operational necessity to do so, for example, to collect a takeaway for their refreshment break.

Should a parking fine be issued to a police vehicle, or a private vehicle being used for police purposes, the payment of such a fine will be the responsibility of the driver.

Taking Vehicles Home

- Police Authority Vehicles will be parked on Police premises overnight. This does not apply to hire vehicles or senior officers/staff personal leased vehicles.
- The only exception will be when authorised by the Department Head/ Superintendent for a specific policing purpose.
- If such authorisation is granted it will not be acceptable for an individual to go on to use the vehicle for personal use. (Except force provided lease cars and Fleet cars WITH THE AUTHORISATION OF THE DEPARTMENT HEAD and vehicles provided for specific on-call duty, such as SFC/TFC, used in support of that on-call role).
- Vehicles can only be parked at alternative locations where there is an explicit benefit to the Force and this must not be undertaken merely for individual driver benefit or convenience.
- Fleet vehicles can be parked at a home address when the driver is on an official on-call Rota (this must be documented).
- Fleet vehicles include unmarked police vehicles with response capability which support the functionality of certain on call roles i.e. Drones, Supt Cadre, SFC, TFC.

- Fleet vehicles can only be parked at stations other than the normal place of work for the benefit of Force requirements in the following circumstances:
  - ➢ If a central location for pooling vehicles is of benefit operationally. It must be documented that the pool is operating in a controlled manner for the benefit of the Force.
  - ➢ Where the safety of the vehicle and equipment would be compromised if parked at the normal place of work.
  - ➢ Expediency is cited. This means that to travel first to normal place of work prior to attending meeting, training etc, from home address would not be of benefit to the Force.

NB: Short term hire vehicles may be taken to home address if expediency applies, but this does not apply to fleet or long-term hire vehicles.

An example of expediency purpose – member of staff lives in Devizes, normal place of work is Salisbury, needs to attend a meeting at Swindon:

> Devizes to Salisbury = 25 miles, Salisbury to Swindon = 44 miles
> Total = 69 miles
> Devizes to Swindon = 25 miles
> Total = 25 miles

Where staff park a vehicle overnight at their home address or at a police station other than their duty station, this must be authorised by the Head of Department or their authorised representative.

These records will be used to show that the legislation is complied with. The vehicle cannot be used for private use other than the journey to and from home to place of work/incident. (Except force provided lease cars and cars which are provided for specific on call duty). Failure to adhere to this requirement could create a personal tax liability which staff will be required to pay.

Where staff are asked to drive a vehicle to a central pool, another station or home address, this does not have to be during duty time to qualify as business use.

Stopping Vehicles

- Officers trained and authorised to stop vehicles should do so in accordance with their training.
- Safety will be a prime consideration in the particular circumstances as will reassurrance where this is necessary - see "vulnerable motorists" below.

Vulnerable Motorists - Stopping

The following advice is supported by NPCC.

Police officers on patrol in uniform in marked police vehicles provide a high level of visible reassurance to the public. That level of reassurance is diminished when an unmarked car is being used and police officers need to take this into account.

If police officers in uniform in an unmarked car have cause to stop any motorist at any time, then they will attract the attention of the driver by the activation and display of blue flashing lights and would flash their headlamps. The driver of the police vehicle or passenger will give a clear indication that they require the driver to pull over and stop. The police driver should consider the use of a siren to assist in attracting the attention of the driver to the presence of the police vehicle, although this would not be done as a matter of course (very often it isn't necessary).

If the occupant of the vehicle is a lone female or male and is worried about the authenticity of the police vehicle, and genuinely feels vulnerable - then the advice to the public is that unless they are 100% certain it is the police, do not stop.

They are instead advised to

- drive steadily to the nearest public place (for example a petrol station where they are open till late, a police station, or somewhere there are a lot of people) and then stop.

- Try to signal to the police that they have acknowledged the request to stop and indicate the action they are taking (eg put their indicator or hazard warning lights on or signal by pointing from the driver's window etc).

- Not to drive off at great speed, or exceed the speed limit thereby making the police think they are trying to get away.

- Keep the doors locked until they are happy it is the police.

- Have their mobile at hand if they have one just in case. They can ask to see a warrant card, which should carry a name and photograph, through the closed window.

- If the driver has a mobile phone then they can call 999 and ask to be connected to the police, who will be happy to confirm the authenticity of the police vehicle and its occupants (or otherwise). An alternative number is 112 - which is a continental alternative to 999. If the mobile phone has no signal it will nevertheless sometimes indicate "emergency calls only" in which case these numbers will still work.

- It is stressed that if using a mobile then hands free should be used. However there is an exemption under the law for someone to use their mobile if they are "using the telephone to call the police, fire, ambulance or other emergency service on 112 or 999".

- If police officers are in an unmarked police vehicle that does not have blue lights and sirens and the officer has cause to want the motorist to stop, then they should summon help from the nearest marked police unit.

Use of Lights on Police Motorcycles

Chief Constables were advised by the Personnel Management Committee on 20th October 2000 that the advice contained at the time within the:

> - Driving Standards Agency Manual for Motorcyclists
> - The Highway Code, and
> - 'Other research material'

recommends all motorcycle training on the public road be conducted during daylight hours with either front or dipped headlights switched on.

Additionally, it was felt the use of headlights on motorcycles at all times appears not only to be sound advice in respect of training, but also in respect of the operational use of police motorcycles, with the possible exception of surveillance drivers.

Rule 86 from the current edition of the Highway Code in respect of daylight riding states "Make yourself as visible as possible from the side as well as the front and rear. You could wear a light or brightly coloured helmet and fluorescent clothing or strips. Dipped headlights, even in good daylight, may also make you more conspicuous. However, be aware that other vehicle drivers may still not have seen you, or judged your distance or speed correctly, especially at junctions".
Force procedure is:

Where the force conduct its own motorcycle training on the public road, front or dipped beam lights will be switched on.

Where motorcycle training of officers is conducted by officers from another force (which may occasionally occur), the use of lights will be a matter for that force/their DTU. The expectation however, is that the advice above will be followed.

In respect of operational duties except surveillance work, either dipped beam or day riding lights (where fitted) will be switched on during daylight hours.

It is recognised however, that night time riding is an essential part of motorcycle courses to meet modern day operational policing requirements. It provides practical, effective training, including risk appreciation in an environment students will regularly find themselves exposed to and working in, on a daily basis.

In respect of surveillance work, the use of lights as above is positively encouraged, particularly now that many motorcyclists use their lights on the roads and it has become the 'norm' amongst the motorcycling public. However, it is recognised the nature of surveillance work requires some flexibility on this issue.

Therefore if, in the opinion of the individual police motorcyclist, the use of either a dipped beam or day riding light may compromise their position in regard to the particular surveillance task in hand, then that police motorcyclist may decide to have their lights switched off. He or she should turn the lights back on again as soon as the need not to have them on changes. It is for the individual trained police motorcylist to risk assess and manage this themselves.

Use of M4 - Non Motorway (Level 3) Trained Officers/Staff

In response to queries raised periodically:

- The M4 may be used by staff who possess a driving permit minimum classification of 1, if it is considered to be the most direct/sensible/easiest/economical route, e.g., to travel from Chippenham to an appointment at Gable Cross.

Standard response trained drivers may use the M4 as above in non emergency response mode to get to their destination. They may also use the M4 in response mode - if the matter is considered by the driver to be one of urgent operational necessity and the M4 is judged by the driver to be the most effective route to the (non motorway) incident at the time. They may **not** engage in pursuits on the motorway.

In order for drivers to be deployed to routinely patrol or deal with incidents on the motorway itself, they must be Motorway (Level 3) trained. This provides them with the necessary training to equip them to work safely in that environment.

If a non Motorway (Level 3) trained officer/member of staff using the motorway encounters a situation that requires police action - they will call that in to the ECC who will task suitably trained staff from Specialist Operations to respond and deal. It is appreciated that in an emergency, eg, someone trapped in a vehicle, they may decide they have to act to save life, but this is no different to any untrained member of the public intervening in such a situation and attempting to help as best they can.

In summary:

> **If you are not trained with either fast roads motorway or the full motorway course you are not to operate on the motorway. This does not stop officers travelling on the motorway network, but if not trained, officers are not to respond to incidents.**

> **If whilst using the motorway, non trained officers come across an incident the following advice is to be followed:**

> > Stop on the hard shoulder, if safe and able to do so.
> > Report the location immediately, giving the number on the marker post.
> > Wear high visibility clothing.
> > Assist with the accident as if you were a member of the public.
> > Do not place yourself in danger and do not attempt to cross the carriageway if traffic is still flowing.
> > Perform the function of a link to the Force Control Room.
> > Do not be forced into action due to frustration or pressure; remember you are untrained and ill equipped to work within this environment.

Only advanced trained drivers who are current TPAC trained, driving high powered tactical grade vehicles, are authorised and suitably equipped to deal with pursuits on the motorway.

Responding to incidents on the strategic road network (SRN)

In addition to the guidance relating to the motorway above, the following refers to the SRN. The SRN is basically the larger roads with no posted speed limit, including dual carriageways where vehicles are travelling faster and there is a greater level of risk involved to those officers attending incidents. This is why there are specific levels of training to be able to deal with particular types of road.

Within there are 3 levels of training delivered to allow officers to respond to deal with incidents on the roads:

Level 1 refers to basic drivers who can attend and deal with incidents on A and B roads with a speed limit below 50, all other roads regardless of speed limits but not dual carriageways and motorways

Level 2 refers to standard drivers who are trained to attend incidents on A roads and dual carriageways regardless of speed limits.

Level 3 refers to advanced drivers who are trained to attend incidents on the motorway.
A "level 3" trained driver can attend any incident, but a level 1 driver can only attend an incident within their area of training. Similarly a level 2 driver can deal with incidents in their level of training and that of level 1.

Police drivers must not perform tasks which are beyond their level of training, and if they are asked to do so should inform the control room of this point.

Level 2 and level 3 drivers will only be Police officers. The nature of the incidents being attended on blue lights are such that they will require warranted powers and the use of exemptions to allow them to reach a scene and effectively manage what they find.

MEDICAL STANDARDS – DRIVERS as per Police Driving APP

Individual Responsibility - All Staff

The force has a legal responsibility and a duty to implement and manage responsibly and effectively
- a safe system of work
- health & safety and
- occupational road risk (driving at or in connection with work).

All police employees who drive their own private vehicles

- to and from work and/or
- in connection with their work
- or who drive police authority owned or hired vehicles in connection with their work

have a legal responsibility to ensure they do not drive when they have a medical condition that should have been declared to DVLA and has not been. Failure to notify DVLA is a criminal offence.

No member of staff should drive in contravention of professional medical advice received.

Diabetic Drivers

The advice referred to above (page 31 of the DVLA document and compliant with FOM guidelines 2013) says "The Secretary of State's Honorary Medical Advisory Panel on Diabetes and Driving has recommended that drivers with insulin treated diabetes should not drive emergency vehicles. This takes account of the difficulties for an individual, regardless of whether they may appear to have exemplary glycaemic control, in adhering to the monitoring processes required when responding to an emergency situation".

"Caveat: The advice of the Panels on the interpretation of EC and UK legislation, and its appropriate application, is made within the context of driver licensing and the DVLA process. It is for others to decide whether or how those recommendations should be interpreted for their own areas of interest, in the knowledge of their specific circumstances".

Force policy in light of the above, is that the Medical Advisory Panel's advice will be followed.
For the sake of clarity this will be applied in force as follows:

- Anyone with insulin treated diabetes will not be permitted to perform any role which requires exercising legal exemptions eg speed exemptions, and/or driving in emergency response mode (whether in uniform or not). This will apply for example, to response, RPU, ARG, and some surveillance /dedicated crime team roles.

  This is a sensible proportionate and justifiable policy control measure in light of the advice issued by the Secretary of State's Medical Advisory Panel.

- Insulin treated drivers affected by the above will be downgraded to Police Basic Level and referred to Occupational Health for an Individual Medical Risk Assessment (IMRA).

- Any other officer or member of staff with insulin treated diabetes whose role requires them to drive whilst at work for any reason, whether police authority owned vehicles, hire vehicles or their own private vehicle, (no matter how infrequently), will also be referred to Occupational Health for an (IMRA).

  Findings from IMRA's, together with any recommendations from the FME will be referred to Line Management for consideration and a decision in the individual circumstances, as to their suitability to drive at work ie work related driving. HR advice may be taken in appropriate cases.

  IMRA's will normally specify or recommend whether further reviews are necessary and if so the frequency.

  If in a particular instance, it is felt further professional medical information, advice or clarification is required by management, Occupational Health must be consulted.

  In the case of insulin treated diabetes, until the result of an IMRA is known, the officer or member of staff will not drive whilst at work.

Eyesight Tests

For standard emergency response drivers and above, this test will comply with the Group 2 Medical Standard as published by the DVLA, or any such standard that may replace it in future.

Medical Fitness to Drive - Concerns

Any concern over the medical fitness of an officer holding, or intending to hold, a standard or advanced driving permit, or any other employee who drives at work, must be brought to the attention of Occupational Health who will consider the need to refer the matter to the Force Medical Officer for adjudication.

GRADED RESPONSES: CCC

Introduction

The Force operate a procedure within CCC whereby incidents are graded in terms of the urgency of the required police response. These take account of national Call Handling Standards for incident grading.

Information

Attached to some of these categories are "target response times" for police arrival at the scene. Performance against these targets is measured.

Driver and Public Safety

The over-riding need is to ensure the safety of the public, police officers and police staff at all times. This particularly applies to situations where an emergency response call is being answered and risks are heightened. It is far better to arrive at the scene safely and be in a position to render assistance, than not to arrive at all. **Drivers of police vehicles can never be indifferent to the safety of the public** and owe a duty of care to other road users as well as to themselves and their passengers. Any failure to maintain a safe, acceptable standard of driving could alongside other action, give rise to:

- ➤ criminal prosecution
- ➤ an action for negligence and
- ➤ liability for damages

Clearly, police drivers have a duty to attend the scene of an emergency call promptly where, in extreme cases, they may be required to help save human life. However, the achievement of a graded response call time will not take precedence over personal and public safety whilst en route.

Under no circumstances will the safety of the public be put in jeopardy by having to meet response targets.

Drivers will, at all times, consider the prevailing conditions and not take unnecessary, disproportionate risks. They should bear in mind they could ultimately be held individually accountable for their actions, possibly in the spotlight of subsequent investigation and /or legal proceedings.

USE OF EMERGENCY EQUIPMENT AND EMERGENCY RESPONSE

Police vehicles are equipped with Emergency Equipment (blue lights and sirens) to allow appropriately trained and certified police officers and staff to perform certain tasks.

These tasks include;

- To notify the driver of a vehicle that the Police want them to stop.
- To allow the emergency vehicle to drive through traffic in order to attend an emergency in a timely fashion.
- To notify other road users of an obstruction or other danger in the road.
- In circumstances where it is justified, appropriate and proportionate to utilise blue lights and sirens to achieve a policing purpose

The decision to use and justify the use of Emergency equipment always rests with the driver of the vehicle.

Depending on the task a certain level of training and certification will be required in order to undertake emergency response. For example, a basic trained driver can use emergency equipment to notify a driver to stop, and to notify other road users of an obstruction. Only a standard or advanced driver can use emergency equipment to make their way through traffic.

The decision of the driver should be based on the following principles;

- Is the use of the emergency equipment Proportionate? *Are we using a sledgehammer to crack a nut?*

- Is the use of the emergency equipment Legitimate? *Going to an injury RTC is one thing – getting home for lunch is another.*

- Is the use of the emergency equipment Accountable? *Rationale for the use of emergency equipment and emergency response should be recorded on a command and control log or in a PNB entry.*

- Is the use of the emergency equipment Necessary? *Can the task be carried out another way?*

If these questions are answered suitably then the use of emergency equipment would likely be considered appropriate.

RESPONDING TO EMERGENCIES

Essential Knowledge

There are no legal exemptions for police drivers to drive at a speed or in a manner which amounts to dangerous driving or driving without due care and attention.

A speed exemption does not sanction negligent driving, nor does it indemnify a negligent driver of a vehicle on an emergency response run against civil liability. The duty of the driver to take care remains undiminished.

Irrespective of the urgency, consider the public perception of your actions behind the wheel. Your training equips you to make progress to your destination - professionally and safely. Do not drive beyond your capabilities, skills or training. If you do then you are exposing yourself and the public to unnecessary danger as well as exposing yourself to potential legal or disciplinary processes.

It is always better to arrive safely than not at all - see section above on Graded Responses.

To drive in an emergency response role using blue lights and sirens, and be eligible to claim speed limit exemptions, drivers **must** be at least standard level with a current minimum driver training classification of 5.

"Current authorised standard response" - means the driver has either successfully passed a standard response driving course in the last 5 years or, has successfully completed a standard response driving refresher in the last 5 years or, the advanced driving equivalent of either of the above.

Response cars will normally be marked (liveried). In some cases they may be unmarked at the discretion of the Fleet Manager. Response duties should be performed in marked response vehicles where possible to reduce risks to all concerned by maximising visibility to other road users. Unmarked response vehicles should not be routinely used where marked response vehicles are available.

Drivers should be aware that the activation of blue lights and sirens does not entitle them to exceed speed limits. Neither does it afford them precedence over other road users. They are ancillary warning devices only - to alert other road users to the presence of the police vehicle on the public road in circumstances that the driver deems to be an emergency.

Even with emergency warning equipment activated, never assume the public are aware of the police vehicle's presence.

The decision to claim an exemption from posted speed limits is a decision for the driver to make, based upon the individual circumstances of the incident they have been tasked to attend, deal with, or have encountered. This decision must be proportionate, legal, accountable, necessary and the least intrusive to achieve the desired outcome, ie, it must be justifiable.

Currently (at the time this procedure was written), statutory speed exemptions are provided by Section 87 of the Road Traffic Regulation Act 1984. Following the implementation of Section19 of the Road Safety Act 2006, police officers and members of police staff **cannot** claim speed exemptions **unless** they have been trained to drive at high speed. For the police service this means current authorised standard response level drivers as a minimum.

USE OF MOBILE PHONES AND POLICE RADIOS WHILST DRIVING

Introduction

1.1 The law requires that drivers **MUST** exercise proper control of their vehicle at all times. Contravention of this requirement is an endorsable offence as is the use of hand-held mobile phones or similar devices whilst driving. The consequences however, may be far more serious if a collision occurs as a result.

1.2 'Similar devices' include any hand-held device that permits two-way communication whether the medium is speech, text or other forms of data. The legislation does not apply to hands-free two-way radio systems however but see 'Police Radios' below.

1.3 Under the legislation, the road traffic act definition of 'driving' applies. This includes when the engine is running and the vehicle is stationary, e.g. at traffic lights or in short hold-ups on the road.

1.4 Hands-free equipment may be used but see provisions 2.3 - 2.6 below.

1.5 None of what follows absolves drivers using equipment from driving with due care and attention, with reasonable consideration for other road users or being in proper control of their vehicle at all times. Drivers are ultimately responsible for their individual actions.

Mobile Phones

2.1 Using a hand-held mobile phone whilst driving is an illegal activity which also places the driver, passengers and other road users at unnecessary risk. Furthermore the public will look to police drivers to set the right example to others at all times. The use of a hand held mobile phone whilst driving is not permitted and, in all cases drivers will find a safe place to stop and switch off their engine before answering or making a call.

2.3 Under the law, a 'hands-free' mobile phone (or police radio) does not require the driver to significantly alter their position in relation to the steering wheel to use it. Conversation using hands-free equipment still however distract attention from the road. It is safer not to use any telephone while you are driving.

2.4 It is acknowledged that using a hands-free mobile phone, fixed for example into a cradle, including pressing buttons in order to make or receive a call (**but not text**) will not specifically breach the regulation. Equally, the force has an obligation to effectively manage and reduce "at work" risks. **Force policy is that the use of a hands-free mobile phone whilst driving is only permitted to the extent necessary to answer a call.** This **does not** mean drivers must answer a hands free mobile call when driving. That is a matter at the particular time for individual judgement and responsibility, but if a call is answered conversation will be very brief. Inform the caller you are driving and never enter into lengthy conversation whilst that is the case. Find a safe place to stop before continuing the conversation or replying to the call.

2.5 Consideration should be given by the driver where practicable, to switching their mobile phone off and planning stops or breaks to deal with any calls. In a non operational policing environment this is more likely to be practicable, but again it is a matter for individual judgement and responsibility in the particular circumstances. It is reiterated however, that the law must be complied with at all times.

2.6 When telephoning a colleague who is driving, both the caller and the driver share a responsibility to manage the risks and comply with this policy. It should be remembered that

- the caller cannot see what the driver can see
- the loss of concentration involved in lengthy and demanding conversations is dangerous for the driver and for other road users, and
- there is a difference between a driver talking to a passenger and talking on the phone. Passengers act as a second set of eyes, and can see when the driver needs to respond to potential hazards.

Police Radios

3.1 The Department for Transport (DfT) have recently changed their stance on the use of hand held radios going back on previous advice that 2 way radio communication was not viewed in the same way as using a hand held mobile phone.

3.2 The use of hands free Airwave radio built into the vehicle is of course permitted. This could be, for example, use of a mains radio set with handset, or a pocket phone in a harness where the driver must 'press to talk' with a remote PTT. Airwave radios used in mobile phone mode will come within the category of a mobile phone and will **not** be used hand-held whilst driving (policy in relation to mobile phones above, will apply).

3.3 Drivers **must** use hands-free radio rather than hand held radios to reduce risk. There is **no exemption from driving whilst using a hand held mobile phone and the latest advice from DfT and the Home Office is that Airwave handheld radios also fall within the same mobile phone legislation. Driving without due care and attention as well as mobile phone legislation still applies to Police officers and Staff.**

3.4 If double-crewed, the driver should not need to use any radio whilst driving.

Emergency Response or Pursuit Situations

4.1 There is a clear need to balance the force's responsibility to investigate offences, suspected offences and answer emergency calls - but not to place any person at unnecessary risk.

4.2 The force and individual staff themselves are accountable for matters arising as a consequence of emergency response or pursuit incidents. **These are high risk activities.** Our duty of care extends to:

- The public
- Offenders and suspected offenders and
- Police employees

4.3 Actions by staff individually must, at all times, be legal, proportionate, relevant and necessary. The safety of all concerned is of paramount importance.

4.4 The standard of driving by police officers must always be beyond reproach if they are to set a proper example and gain and maintain respect and co-operation of the public, which is essential.

4.5 In pursuit situations where commentary is required, the driver will only give the commentary if they are single-crewed, or if their passenger is untrained.

4.6 Appropriately trained officers will be aware the driving task will come 'first' and commentary 'second' - and safety will be the over-riding consideration for all concerned.

VEHICLE LOG BOOKS AND VEHICLE CHECKS

Log Books Completion - Procedure

No doubt must exist as to the identity of a driver from log book details on any given time or date.

Log books contain instructions on their completion and will be kept in the vehicle to which they have been allocated.

Before leaving the station, drivers will if practicable, enter date, name, rank and number in the vehicle log book.

Upon completion of the journey, drivers will complete the log book entry, including the route or nature of duty undertaken. Oil and fuel issues will also be entered.

Log books will be examined weekly by a supervisory officer with particular attention paid to their proper completion and the purposes for which vehicles have been used.

Log Books will be used where necessary to assist in any investigation.

When completed (full), log books must be forwarded to Fleet & Services Department for records/ retention.

The following was previously published in General Orders and still applies: "It is evident that the practice amongst many officers of all ranks has been not to record details of driver changeover during a tour of duty.

The Assistant Chief Constable has instructed this practice will cease forthwith. When drivers change over, the appropriate entry, including the time and date, will be entered in the log book at that time. Entries will be legible.

All drivers have a responsibility to ensure they make accurate and complete entries and the vehicle log book is up-to-date. No doubt should exist as to the identity of a driver from log book details at a later date.

Officers who do not comply with this order may be the subject of discipline procedures. Supervisors are reminded they have a duty to examine log books weekly and particular attention should be paid to the proper completion of entries".

Vehicle Log Books - Hire Vehicles

Following a guidance note issued by ACPO on the legal obligations placed on forces as a 'Body Corporate' when dealing with speeding and red light offences by emergency vehicles, there is now also a legal obligation to record all drivers of hire vehicles and details of their journey.

Subsection 5 of section 172 (Road Traffic Act 1988) provides that where the offence is by a body corporate and is due to the consent, connivance or neglect of a director, manager etc, then that person as well as the body corporate may be guilty of an offence.

This in short means the force must be able to identify the individual using that vehicle at the time the offence was committed, otherwise the responsibility of that offence can be directed at a manager, or director that has had dealings with that vehicle.

In order for the force to identify the driver in such cases, **all hire vehicles must carry a force log book.** The log book contains all the relevant details and responsibilities required by the driver in connection with any journey carried out on behalf of the force.

All vehicles hired must be insured by informing the Fleet and Services department of the date of hire (both on and off), the make and model of the vehicle hired, and where possible the name of the driver or drivers. Any collision occurrences must be reported immediately.

Daily and Weekly Vehicle Checks/Inspections

These checks are an important control measure in managing the risks to both personal and public safety associated with the operation of police vehicles on the public highway. Every individual who drives a police vehicle has a personal responsibility, as do their supervisors, to ensure they are:

- safe to use
- not used illegally with defects, eg with defective lights or tyres and, where applicable,
- equipment, (including HOSTYDS) is present and in a serviceable condition.

It is **not** acceptable to fail in relation to the above.

Daily Vehicle Checks

These will be completed before using a police vehicle unless due to an immediate emergency response call it is not possible to do so, in which case the driver will complete the check as soon as practicable during their tour of duty.

Ensure the vehicle log book has been completed in respect of the previous journey.

Carry out visual inspection of the vehicle, including the condition of the tyres. Immediately report any damage or defect found to a supervisor.

Check and replenish where necessary, fuel, engine oil, water in the radiator and windscreen washer fluid. If visual inspection suggests tyre pressures may not be correct or if any doubt exists, tyre pressures **will** be physically checked immediately.

From a practical viewpoint, it is accepted that actual tyre pressures will not be checked by officers each day. However, they will be checked **without fail** at least once a week and to ensure this does happen, tyre pressures **will be checked as part of the weekly inspection.**

Ensure lights, indicators and windscreen wipers are in good order. Ensure lights are clean.

> Unmarked police vehicles: As part of vehicle POWDER checks, please ensure that you check all blue lights (in addition to any other vehicle lights) to ensure that they have not been concealed in any way.
>
> *[If there is an operational requirement to conceal blue lights (or any other vehicle lights) then you notify your Inspector about this. Please note that any such practice will need to be accompanied by a risk assessment and a justification as to why such a practice is operationally necessary].*

Ensure a reasonable standard of interior and exterior cleanliness consistent with prevailing conditions.

Satisfy yourself all equipment carried in or on the vehicle is in good order, properly stowed and safe.

Check warning instrumentation within the vehicle when the ignition is switched on. If a warning light is illuminated indicating a possible problem, ensure this is acted upon and resolved.

Take the opportunity when pulling away, to test brakes and steering appear to be working correctly.
At the completion of each tour of duty, drivers of all police vehicles will:

- Re-fuel the vehicle
- Report any damage or defect to a supervisor if not already reported. Record details in log book.
- Ensure vehicle log book entry for tour of duty is accurate and complete.

Weekly Vehicle Checks

These checks are **not** optional. They support daily checks and constitute an important control measure in managing "at work" risk. They will be recorded in vehicle logbooks as a matter of both health & safety and (in particular, given our role as an emergency service), responsible management of occupational road risk.

At least once a week, a thorough vehicle inspection will take place which will involve checking:

➢ all items forming part of the daily vehicle check above.
➢ in particular tyre condition - a pressure check **will** be carried out as part of this.
➢ the presence and condition of the vehicle equipment (including HOSTYDS).

Where practicable and available, it is good practice for a supervisory officer to assist with the checks and complete the certificate on pages 31/32 of the vehicle log book. If a supervisory officer is not available, the officer conducting the check will sign the log book themselves. They will ensure entries are legible.

The Fleet Manager reserves the right to call in log books for checking at any time.

No alternations/additions/modifications will be made to any police vehicle or its equipment without the authority of the Fleet and Services Manager. No adjustments to the vehicle will be made except by a properly qualified mechanic appropriately authorised to do it.

VEHICLE DEFECTS

• All defects, however slight, must be reported promptly by the driver to a supervisory officer, who will inform Workshops at CCO. Form 124 is designed for this purpose and should be used.

• Where it is considered the defect or suspected defect would render the use of the vehicle unsafe or illegal, the vehicle will be withdrawn from use until any necessary repairs have been carried out. Particular attention will be paid to brakes, steering and tyres.

Further detailed operating procedure surrounding for example, vehicle care, maintenance, service, breakdowns and cleaning is the responsibility of the Fleet and Services Department and is not covered here. Details can be found on Firstpoint. Please contact Fleet and Services Department or Vehicle Workshops as appropriate in the event of a query.

Notes:

Notes:

Notes:

Notes:

Notes:

Notes:

Notes:

Notes:

Notes:

Notes:

Notes:

Notes:

Notes:

Notes:

Notes:

Notes:

Notes:

Notes:

Notes:

Notes:

Notes:

Notes:

Notes:

Printed in Great Britain
by Amazon

45581270R00044